MOON SPELL MAGIC

INVOCATIONS, INCANTATIONS & LUNAR LORE FOR A HAPPY LIFE

Cerridwen Greenleaf

author of *The Witches' Love Spell Book*

Cover, Layout & Design: Laura Mejía

For permission requests, please contact the publisher at:
Mango Publishing Group
2850 Douglas Road, 3rd Floor
Coral Gables, FL 33134 USA
info@mango.bz

For special orders, quantity sales, course adoptions and corporate sales, please email the publisher at sales@mango.bz. For trade and wholesale sales, please contact Ingram Publisher Services at customer.service@ingramcontent.com or +1.800.509.4887.

MOON SPELL MAGIC:
Invocations, Incantations & Lunar Lore for a Happy Life

Library of Congress Cataloging
Names: Cerridwen Greenleaf
Title: Moon Spell Magic / by Cerridwen Greenleaf
Library of Congress Control Number: 2017901658
ISBN 9781633535626 (paperback), ISBN 9781633535633 (eBook)
BISAC Category Code: OCC026000 BODY, MIND & SPIRIT/Witchcraft

ISBN: (paperback) 978-1-63353-562-6, (ebook) 978-1-63353-563-3
Printed in the United States of America

This book is for my teachers, wise women and men who led me to the moonlit path.

Hear the words of the Star Goddess,
the dust of whose feet are the hosts of heaven,
whose body encircles the universe:
I who am the beauty of the green earth and the white moon
among the stars and the mysteries of the waters,
I call upon your soul to arise and come unto me.
For I am the soul of nature that gives life to the universe.
From Me all things proceed and unto Me they must return.

Anonymous,
The Charge of the Goddess

Moon Spell Magic: Invocations, Incantations and Lunar Lore for a Happy Life.

This book is intended to be a practical and inspirational handbook to making magic—from spells for each day of the week, rituals for romance, seasonal sacred energy altars, secrets for money magic, and everything in between. *Moon Spell Magic* will contain an abundance of folk wisdom, as well as many modern pagan practices that will help readers learn the necessary lore and background information for creating the life of their dreams. Rituals and incantations can lead to great personal growth. Witches are among the most devoted spiritual seekers, and this book can be an important tool for just this, adding a deep grounding in magical correspondences, astrological associations, and the myths behind the magic. Whether you are looking to conjure up a supernatural Saturday for your coven or rid your home of negative energy and blocks to happiness, this numinous guide can help readers turn their homes into personal pagan power centers while having fun in the process. The moon has enormous power and celestial energy; by harnessing that, you can improve your life every day with the spells in this book.

Table of Contents

Introduction

Using the Night Sky As Your Guide

For centuries, witches have known that luck is neither random nor mysterious. Thanks to the wise women in my family who shared their "trade secrets" openly, I learned very early in life my fate was mine to guide, and I could manifest my will through the tools of magic. I have never used witchcraft specifically to get money, but I have used it to find a good home, attract job opportunities, and help others. People have always marveled at what they perceive as my "good luck," or suggested I have a fleet of guardian angels behind my every move. But luck and angels have nothing to do with it.

As soon as you approach your magic consciously, you will see you have the power to choose abundance. And when you increase your material prosperity, you reduce the need to worry about such worldly matters. Only then you can move on to achieving true prosperity: pursuing your pleasures, spending time with family and friends, and enjoying your life. Magic and spellwork is about expansion – expanding your horizons, enriching your mind and spirit, celebrating the real riches of health and happiness. Every witch walks her spiritual path with practical feet and is aware of the fiercely competitive world in which we live. With life's increasingly frantic pace, the search for serenity is now more important than ever. Herein lay the keys to rising above the fray and embracing a life of abundance and joy.

Every day is an opportunity for growth in every aspect of your life, and its level of success is entirely up to you. Think of these as pagan prescriptions for the twenty-first century, guaranteed to banish stress, ease tension, and add comfort, joy and magic to your daily life. Blessed be!

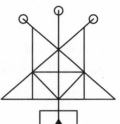

Chapter 1:

The Lunar Calendar: Spells for Every Phase of the Moon

The proper phase of the moon is essential for spell craft. The waning moon is the time to wind down any personal challenges and see them to an end. The new moon is an auspicious time for a fresh start. While waxing, the moon grows steadily larger and is good for spellwork toward fruition. The full moon is a great teacher with a special message for each month. The moon moves through the wheel of the zodiac from sign to sign every two to three days.

Performing a spell at the optimal time in the lunar cycle will maximize your power. As you read the spells in this book, keep this elemental magic in mind:

Each lunar cycle begins with a "new" phase, when the moon lies between the sun and the earth so the illuminated side cannot be seen.. The moon gradually "waxes" until it has moved to the opposite side of the earth, its lit side faceing us in the "full" moon phase. It then begins to "wane" until it reaches the New Moon phase again. The entire cycle takes a month, during which the moon orbits the earth. To determine the sun sign governing the

moon, you will need a celestial guide or almanac. My favorite is *Llewellyn's Daily Planetary Guide.*

New Moon Flower Power

This flower-infused potpourri is wonderful for clearing the way for the new in your life and planting "seeds" for new moon beginnings. You can also create a wreath with garlic bulbs for self-protection and insurance that your newly laid plans won't go awry.

Flower ingredients:

• Rose

• Snapdragon

• Marigold

• Carnation

Place the flowers in a bowl and then sprinkle them with a few drops of geranium, clove, and cinnamon oil. Place the mixture on the south point of your altar for the duration of a full lunar cycle, from new moon to new moon.

New Moon Spells

We all know about the power of full moon spells, but don't neglect the energy of the other moon phases. New moon spells can be quite powerful as long as you target the right purposes during this time of the lunar cycle.

The new moon is the time for beginnings and new projects, so this is a good time to work some magick towards a new path in your life. Needless to say, cast these spells during a new moon phase.

Seeding the Future – New Moon Ritual

What are your intentions for the coming months? What you can imagine, you can bring into being. This ritual will aid you in getting what you want and need for yourself and loved ones. Nothing says "new beginnings" like planting a seed, so use the power of a growing plant to bring success to your own new moon projects. Assemble the following:

- A flowerpot filled halfway with soil

- Enough soil to fill the pot

- Seeds (nasturtiums are oh-so-easy to grow)

- Egg shells

- A small piece of paper

Get everything together and write your intentions on the paper in as few words as possible and roll into a scroll. Place the scroll in the pot, and then crush some egg shells on top of that. Fill the rest of the pot with soil.

Repeat the following:

I plant this seed when the moon is new,
Manifest my intentions, I ask it true. So mote it be.

Keep repeating this as you plant your seeds, and give them a little water. After the ritual, keep the pot somewhere sunny and you should start seeing some success in your plans when the plant begins to sprout. Keep it healthy and thriving to keep the magic going. You can perform a ritual like this anytime you feel the need and the moon is new. You can also be very specific in your intentions: new love, an interview for a new job, finding a new home you love. I find that the more specific you are in setting your intentions, the more powerful the spell.

New Job, New Moon

Another good spell purpose for the new moon is getting a new job. If you're seeking new employment, try this ritual out. Get your supplies out:

- 2 green candles

- 2 white candles

- 2 gold candles

- 2 pieces of green jade or another green stone

- Cinnamon oil

Line up the candles, alternating the colors. Anoint each one with cinnamon oil, and rub a little oil on the stones too. Start at one end and light each candle. With each one, repeat these words:

A new career is what I desire,
I cast this spell to get a hire.
By the light of this new moon,
I need a new job soon.

After all the candles are lit, take each stone and gently pass it through the flames (careful of your fingers). Then hold the stones in your hands and visualize the type of job you want to get. After the spell, pocket the stones and carry them with you. You should have a new job by the next new moon.

The Dark Side of the Moon – Eclipse Enchantments

When the moon passes into the Earth's shadow, this is a lunar eclipse. These are rare occasions that make for a truly enchanted evening. I recommend you think ahead to what you want to accomplish in this phase, since an eclipse only lasts several hours. Think about what you want brought out of the shadow and into the light – do you need to dust off old dreams and reactivate them? Do you have old hurts and wounds you need to let go of and purge from your life? Do you feel there is a secret being kept from you? This one night is perfect for the purposes of saying goodbye to the old and ushering in the new. Simply plan your magical workings to coordinate with the passing shadow. When the moon is in full eclipse, treat those few moments as if the moon was in its Dark phase. It is also an excellent time to honor the goddess of the moon in a group or solo ritual. Think through carefully your heart's desire and what will serve you for many months to come.

White Light of Love: A Waning Moon

To light the flower of love in your heart, time this charm for the waning of a New Moon. Place a green candle beside a white lily, rose or freesia. Make sure it is a posy of personal preference. White flowers have the greatest perfume and either of these beauties will impart your home with a pleasing aura. I like to float a gardenia in a clear bowl of fresh water, truly the essence of the divine. Light the candle and hold the flower close to your heart. Pray,

Steer me to the highest light;
guide me to beauty and truth.
Much have I to give.
Much have I to live.
Bright blessings to one and all.

Waning Moon Money Magic

To attract money, fill a big pot with fresh water and place it on your altar during the waxing moon. Pour a cup of milk with a tablespoon of honey and a tablespoon of ground clove into the pot as an offering. Toss handfuls of dried chamomile and mint into the cauldron. Say aloud:

I call upon you, gods and goddesses of old, to fill my purse with gold. I offer you mother's milk and honey sweet.

With harm to none and blessings to thee, I honor you for bringing me health and prosperity.

Place the offering bowl on your altar and leave the aromatic mixture there to instill your kitchen with the energy of abundance. After four hours and forty-four minutes, go outside your home and pour the offering into your kitchen garden or into the roots of a shrub. Then bow in appreciation of the kindness of the gods and goddesses.

Lucky 13 Waxing Moon Spell

Your altar is the heart center of your home, your sanctuary. Yet the world is constantly coming in and bringing mundane energy over your threshold—problems at the workplace, financial woes, bad news from your neighborhood or the world at large. All this negativity wants to get in the way and stay. While you can't do anything about the stock market crash in China or a coworker's divorce, do not allow this bad energy to cling to you. Instead, you can do something about it with a homekeeping spell. The best times to release any and all bad luck is on a Friday the 13th or on any waxing moon. As you know, Friday the 13th is considered a lucky day on the witch's calendar.

Get a big black candle and a black crystal, a piece of white paper, a black pen with black ink and a cancellation stamp, readily available at any stationery store. Go into your backyard or a nearby park or woodlands and find a flat rock that has a slightly concave surface.

Using the pen, write down on the white paper that which you want to rid yourself and your home of; this is your release request. Place the candle and the black crystal on the rock, and light the candle near an open window. As the negativity is released outside while the candle burns, intone:

Waxing moon, most wise Cybele,
From me this burden please dispel
Upon this night so clear and bright
I release ___ to the moon tonight.

Go outside and place the rock altar on the ground and visualize a clear and peaceful home filled with only the positive as the candle burns for thirteen minutes. Stamp the paper with the cancel stamp. Snuff the candle, fold the paper away from your body, and place it under the rock. Speak your thanks to the moon for assisting you. If you have a truly serious issue at hand, repeat the process for thirteen nights and all will be vanquished.

Under a Waxing Moon

When the first narrow crescent of the waxing moon appears in the twilight sky, place a green candle beside a white lily or freesia. White flowers have the most intense aromas. Anoint the candle with tuberose or rose oil. Take a handful of seeds, such as sunflower, walnuts, or pistachios, still in their shells, and place them in front of the candle.

Close your eyes and recite aloud:

Under this darkling moons,
In Eden fair, I walk through flowers
In the garden of my desires,
I light the flame of my mind,
I plant the seeds of things to come.

Safe Haven Potpourri

Potpourri was a medieval product revived by the Victorians, who used the symbolic meanings and powers of flowers. Grow flowers in your kitchen garden or buy cut flowers. Dry them; then place them in a pretty container. Choose flowers that connect with your astrological sun sign, moon sign and personal energy. Try a mix of your favorites along with some of the beloved posies of Victorian and medieval times:

Daisy opens in the morning and closes when the sun goes down; this beloved flower is associated with purity, loyalty, innocence, patience and simplicity.

Pansies are also called Heartsease and represent merriment!

Iris stands for wisdom, faith, friendship and hope eternal.

Floral Healing Remedies

Flower essences mixed with 30 millimeters distilled water can also be used as the following remedies:

- Addiction: skullcap, agrimony

- Anger: nettle, blue flag, chamomile

- Anxiety: garlic, rosemary, aspen, periwinkle, lemon balm, white chestnut, gentian

- Bereavement: honeysuckle

- Depression: borage, sunflower, larch, chamomile, geranium, yerba santa, black cohosh, lavender, mustard

- Exhaustion: aloe, yarrow, olive, sweet chestnut

- Fear: poppy, mallow, ginger, peony, water lily, basil, datura

- Heartbreak: heartsease, hawthorn, borage

- Lethargy: aloe, thyme, peppermint

- Stress: dill, echinacea, thyme, mistletoe, lemon balm

- Spiritual blocks: oak, ginseng, lady's slipper

Blessed Balm Spell
(Waning Moon is Optimal)

Simmer this mixture whenever you feel the need to infuse your home and heart with the energies of protection. A waning moon is the time to banish old negative energy. This will safeguard you and your loved ones from outside influences that could be negative or disruptive. Set your intention and gather together the following herbs:

¼ cup rosemary

1 teaspoon dill weed

4 bay laurel leaves

cup cedar

1 tablespoon basil

1 teaspoon juniper berries

1/8 cup sage

Mix your herbs together by hand. While you are doing this, close your eyes and visualize your home as a sacred place protected by a boundary of glowing white light. Add the herbs to a pan filled with simmering water. When the aromatic steam rises, intone:

By my own hand, I have made this balm;
This divine essence contains my calm.
By my own will, I make this charm;
This precious potpourri protects all from harm.
With harm to none and health to all,
Blessed be!

Blowing in the Wind – A Charm
(Waning Moon is Optimal)

When the moon is waning, this is your opportunity to release anything that no longer serves in your life. We all need to embrace the winds of change in life, clearing away the old and making room for the new. This charm helps overcome upset and can help release anger and grudges. And isn't this an important first step to happiness? What you'll need: a blustery day, access to the outdoors, basil and sage.

Well, it's not mandatory that you have a hill for this, but you do need an open area outside for happiness spells like this. It does need to be windy.

Take your herbs to your spot of choice with your back to the wind. Take the basil and sage and throw them up in the air as you visualize your problems blowing far, far away. Repeat this charm aloud:

No more fear and doubt and pain
Nothing to lose and only joy to gain.
Now, turn around and face into the wind. Speak aloud:
May the winds of change be kind to me
And bring about happiness and glee.
Stress-free and happy I will be

Close your eyes and feel the breeze on your skin and blowing through your hair. Stand still for a few more moments, focused on the release of your problems and the acceptance of peace and the calm that lies ahead in your future.

Spring Full Moon – Invocation of the Flower Moon

This dazzling spring Flower Moon is an optimal opportunity to strive for the new, to initiate a phase of transformation that will last long after the Full Moon has waxed into darkness. This invocation honors the season, planting seeds of positive change in your life to bloom for years to come. Start by gathering red and green apples, candles of the same colors, and seed corn from a gardening store, along with three stalks of lavender and three long strands of night-blooming jasmine. Leave these offerings on your altar all day.

When the Full Moon of May reaches the highest point in the night sky, light one red and one green candle on your kitchen altar. Wind the jasmine and lavender into a crown for the top of your head, breathing in the lovely scent the flowers produce. Holding an apple in each hand, speak this spell while circling the altar clockwise three times.

Moon of Flowers; light the way to change tonight,
Through the power of Earth and Air, Water and Fire.
As I bite this fruit of knowledge, I am thus inspired.
All possibilities are before me. And so it is.

Eat from both apples until you are fully satisfied, and then bury twelve corn seeds and the cores in the rightmost corner of your garden. With the spring rains and summer sun, your intentions will flower into being. By the fall full moon, you will harvest the bounty of change from this spell, with great gratitude.

Lunar Lore – 12 Months of Full Moons

Many of our full moon names come from medieval books of hours and also from the Native American tradition. Here is a list of rare names from the two traditions you may want to use in your lunar rituals.

January: Old Moon, Chaste Moon; this fierce Wolf Moon is the time to recognize your strength of spirit

February: Hunger Moon; the cool Snow Moon is for personal vision and intention-setting

March: Crust Moon, Sugar Moon; the gentle Sap Moon heralds the end of winter and nature's rebirth

April: Sprouting Grass Moon, Egg Moon, Fish Moon; spring's sweet Pink Moon celebrates health and full life force

May: Milk Moon, Corn Planting Moon, Dyad Moon; the Flower Moon provides inspiration with the bloom of beauty

June: Hor Moon, Rose Moon; the Strawberry Moon heralds Summer Solstice and sustaining power of the sun

July: Buck Moon, Hay Moon; this Thunder Moon showers us with rain and cleansing storms

August: Barley Moon, Wyrt Moon, Sturgeon Moon; summer gifts us with the Red Moon, the time for passion and lust for life

September: Green Corn Moon, Wine Moon; fall's Harvest Moon is the time to be grateful and reap what we have sown

October: Dying Grass Moon, Travel Moon, Blood Moon, Moon of Changing Seasons; the Hunter's moon is when we plan and store for winter ahead

November: Frost Moon, Snow Moon; Beaver Moon is the time to call upon our true wild nature

December: Cold Moon, Oak Moon; this is the lightest night of the shortest day and is the time to gather the tribe around the fire and share stories of the good life together

Conjuring Conviviality – a Moon Day Ritual

How you start your week sets the tone for each day to come. It makes a lot of sense to do whatever you can to up the joy quotient for yourself and your loved ones. Jasmine tea is a delightful concoction and can create an aura of bliss and conviviality. It is available at any grocer or purveyor of organic goods but homegrown is even better. Brew a cup of jasmine tea and let it cool. Add two parts lemonade and drink the mixture with a good friend. Jasmine is a vine and represents the intertwining of people. You will be more bonded to anyone with whom you share this sweet ritual. If you grow a night-blooming jasmine vine outside your bedroom window, a heavenly scent will also waft in that creates and enhances an atmosphere of love in your home.

This is also a tonic that you can indulge in alone. I recommend brewing up a batch every Monday, or "Moon Day," to ensure that each week is filled with joyfulness. As the jasmine tea steeps, pray:

On this Moon Day in this new week,
I call upon the spirits to guide joy to my door.
By this moon on this day, I call upon Ishtar and Celene, ladies fair
To show me the best way to live.
For this, I am grateful.
Blessed be the brew; blessed be me.

Dispelling Blocks: Full Moon Incantation

Is something getting in your way? Do you feel stalled out and overcome with procrastination? To overcome any blocks obstructing your creativity and productivity, you can dispel the negative energy by going for a walk in the nearest park. Find a round, flat rock, six to ten inches wide. This will become an altar supplied directly to you by Mother Nature, and it will have the purest energy. Begin by charging this stone on the full moon at your home altar. Light a white candle for purification, and then place your hand on the stone and chant three times:

Bad energy, take flight!
Goddess of Night, shine bright.
Moon of tonight, you give us delight.
Fill this stone with your light,
Imbue it with all your magic and might,
Surround it with your protective sight.
So mote it be.

Ideally, you'll want to perform this spell three times on three consecutive full moons before you begin drawing upon its energy. Like your altar, your stone will be a reservoir you can turn to any time you feel stuck or uninspired. This rock will emanate with a quiet power you can draw from whenever you need.

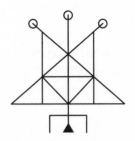

Chapter 2:

Setting Up Your Lunar Altar: Your Personal Power Center

Before there were temples and churches, the primary place for expressing reverence was the altar. The word "altar" comes from a Latin word which means "high place." With a personal altar, you can reach the heights of your spirituality and ascend in wisdom. You construct an altar when you assemble symbolic items in a meaningful manner, focusing both your attention and intention. When you work with the combined energies of these items, you are performing ritual. Your rituals can arise from your needs, imagination, or the seasonal and traditional ceremonies that you find in this book and others. A book I draw much inspiration from has been Nancy Brady Cunningham's *A Book of Women's Altars.* I love her advice to bow or place your hands on the ground in front of your altar at the beginning of ritual work and at the closing, explaining, "Grounding symbolizes the end of the ritual and signals to the mind to return to an ordinary state of awareness as you re-enter daily life." An altar is a physical point of focus for the ritual, containing items considered sacred and essential to ritual work and spiritual growth. An altar can be anything from a rock in the forest to an exquisitely carved antique table. Even portable or temporary altars can suffice such as a board suspended between two chairs for "rituals on the go."

Creating Your Sanctuary Shrine (New Moon Phase is Optimal)

On a low table or chest of your choosing, place a forest green cloth and a brown candle to represent family and home. Add lovely objects you have gathered, including from the garden and outdoors: ocean-carved driftwood, a gorgeous flower, a dried seed pod, a favorite crystal, whatever pleases your eye. It is of the utmost importance to add a bouquet of wildflowers native to your area you gathered close to where you live or bought locally. These posies will help integrate you and your home into your neighborhood and geographic region. Add a sweetly scented sachet of herbs from your kitchen garden or those you intend to plant: rosemary, lavender, thyme, mint, all of which imbue your space with positive energy. Burn associated essential oils, those which will create an aura of comfort around your kitchen, including vanilla, cinnamon, or sweet orange neroli in an oil lamp. Finally, anoint the brown candle while concentrating on the power of peace and bliss surrounding your home and all around your home altar. Chant:

Peace and abundance are in abundance
And here true bliss surrounds
From now on, all disharmony is gone
This is a place of powerful blessings
For here lives sheer joy.
And so it is — blessed be!

This consecrated space will ease your spirits at any time. Your altar connects you to the earth of which you are a part.

Happy Home Spell
(Waning Moon Phase is Optimal)

To anoint your home and turn it into a protective shield for you and your loved ones, rub any of the following essential oils on your doorjambs: cinnamon, clove, dragon's blood, myrrh. Walk through the door into your home and close it securely. Take the remaining essential oils and rub a bit on every other door and window. Light anointed white candles and place them in the windows and chant the words of the spell:

My home is my temple.
Here I love and love,
Safe and secure
Both below and above.
And so it is by magic sealed.

Energy Management: House Blessings
(All Moon Phases)

This magical tool was born centuries ago from the practical magic of sweeping the ritual area clean before casting a spell. With focus and intention, you can dispel negative influences and bad spirits from the area and prepare a space for ritual work. In bygone days, pagan marriages and Beltane trysts took place with a leap over the broom, an old-fashioned tradition of hand fasting, the classic witch wedding. Over the centuries, this rich history combined to capture the imagination as the archetypal symbol of witches.

Your broom is an essential tool for energy management. Obtain a handmade broom from a craft fair or your favorite metaphysical five and dime. This should not be a machine-made plastic one from the supermarket, though I did get a long cinnamon-infused rush broom from Trader Joe's that I use in my witch's kitchen. A broom made of wood and woven of natural straw will be imbued with the inherent energies of those organic materials.

This is very important—do not use your ritual broom for housecleaning. Like me, you may well view every inch of your home as sacred space but you will need to keep your regular housekeeping implements separate from those you will use for your magical workings. Think of it as a separation of church and state, if you will. And, it pretty much is!

In general, it is not advisable to use tools such as your ritual knife to debone a chicken, for example, as this risks a confusing blending of the mundane and magical energies. If you treat your ritual tools with the utmost respect, they will serve you very well. Over time, they will become inculcated with magic through exclusive use in your ritual workings. The Wiccan tradition holds brooms in high regard, and some witches have an impressive collection of brooms, each one named to distinguish their roles as "familiars," or kindred spirits. Kitchen witches often have the most extensive bevy of brooms of anyone.

Moon Mojo: Clear A Space and Make It Yours (Waning Moon is Optimal)

To purify your space with as much of your own personal energy as possible, a broom you have crafted by hand is best. You don't have to wait until you are holding a circle or performing spellcraft; it can be after a squabble with a loved one, to rid yourself of a bout of the blues, or any upset you need to sweep right out of your home. Many a kitchen witch begins the day with this simple ritual of a clean sweep to freshen surroundings and to make room for good energy in your life. This is, of course, not a white glove-type cleaning; it is a symbolic act that is effective in maintaining your home as a personal sanctuary.

You can make your own purification broom from straw bound together and attached to a fallen tree branch, or you can add mojo to a store-bought broom. Wrap copper wire around the bottom of your broom handle and also use it to bind straw to a sturdy stick or branch for the DIY kind. Venus-ruled copper lends an aura of beauty and keeps negativity at bay. Attach crystals to the handle with glue to boost your broom's power. Recommended crystal for space clearing and purification are as follows:

• *Amber* for good cheer

• *Blue Lace Agate* for tranquility and a peaceful home

• *Coral* for wellbeing

• *Jet* absorbs bad energy

• *Onyx* is a stone of protection

- *Petrified Wood* for security

- *Tiger's Eye* will protect you from energy-draining situations or people

- *Turquoise* creates calm and relaxation

Crystal Clear
(New or Waning Moon is Optimal)

Over time, you will doubtless adorn your sacred altar space with many beautiful crystals. Whenever you acquire a new crystal, you need to cleanse it.

Gather these elemental energies:

- A candle for fire

- A cup of water

- Incense for air

- A bowl of salt

Pass your crystal through the scented smoke of the incense and say:

Inspired with the breath of air

Pass the crystal swiftly through the flame of the candle and say:

Burnished by fire

Sprinkle the crystal with water and say:

Purified by water

Dip the crystal into the bowl of salt and say:

Empowered by the earth

Hold the crystal before you with both hands and imagine an enveloping, warm white light purifying the tool. Now say:

Steeped in spirit and bright with light

Place the cleansed crystal upon your altar and say:

By craft made and by craft charged and changed,
This crystal I will use for the purpose of good in this world.
In the realm of the gods and goddesses.
I hereby consecrate this crystal.
Blessings to all, blessed be.

By Jove! A Spell for Wealth (New Moon is Optimal)

On any Thursday or new moon, light your altar candle at midnight and burn frankincense and myrrh incense. Make an offering of a golden fruit, such as apples or peaches, to Jupiter, and anoint your third eye with a corresponding essential oil, such as myrrh, frankincense, apple, or peach.

Pray aloud:

This offering I make as my blessing to all.
Greatest of gods, Lord Jove of the sky.

From you, all heavenly gifts do fall.
Most generous of all, you never deny.
To you, I am grateful, and so mote it be!

Put the candle in a safe, fireproof place, such as a fireplace, and let it burn all night. You will dream of your loved ones, including yourself, receiving a bounty of material and spiritual wealth.

Ritual Herbs: Using Mother Nature's Magic

Refer to this list whenever you are setting up your altar and setting your intention for ritual work.

Benzoin can be used for purification, prosperity, work success, mental acuity, and memory.

Camphor can be used for healing, divining the future, curbing excess, especially romantic obsessions, and a surfeit of sexuality.

Cinnamon refreshes and directs spirituality. It is also handy for healing, money, love, lust, personal power, and success with work and creative projects.

Clove is good for bringing money to you, for protection, for your love life and for helping evade and deter negative energies.

Copal should be used for love and purification.

Frankincense is another spiritual essence that purifies and protects.

Lavender is a plant for happiness, peace, true love, long life and chastity. It is an excellent purifier that aids with sleep.

Myrrh has been considered since ancient times to be deeply sacred. It aids personal spirituality, heals and protects, and can help ward off negative spirits and energies.

Nutmeg is a lucky herb that promotes good health and prosperity and encourages fidelity.

Patchouli stimulates and grounds while engendering both sensuality and encourages fidelity.

Peppermint is an herb of purification, healing, and love. It supports relaxation and sleep as it helps to increase psychic powers.

Rosemary is good for purification, protection, healing, relaxation and intelligence. It attracts love and sensuality, helps with memory, and can keep you youthful.

Sage brings wisdom, purification, protection, health and a long life. It can help make your wishes come true.

Sandalwood is a mystical, healing, protecting essence that helps attract the objects of your hopes and desires and disperses negative energies and spirits.

Star anise is a lucky herb that aids divination and psychism.

Tonka bean brings courage and draws love and money.

Vanilla brings love and enriches your mental capacity.

- Wood aloe is good for dressing or anointing talismans and amulets you want to use for protection.

Peace and Healing Potpourri
(Waxing or Full Moon is Optimal)

Sometimes, we all need a quick fix and this is exactly what this herbal mélange can do for you. Draw some fresh water and simmer this mixture on your stove whenever you feel the need to infuse your space with protection or do an energetic turnaround from negative to positive. A bad day at work, family squabble, an unfortunate incident in your neighborhood: instead of just muddling along, you can do something about it and your creation of the positive will help you and your loved one as well as your neighbors. This powerful potpourri will also safeguard from outside influences that can be disruptive. Set your intention and gather these herbs from your stores:

- 7 cinnamon sticks

- ¼ cup rosemary

- 4 Bay laurel leaves

- 1/8 cup sage

- 1 teaspoons juniper berries

Mix the herbs together by hand. While you are sifting, close your eyes and visualize your home protected by a boundary of glowing white light. Imagine the light running throughout you to the herbs in your hand, charging them with the energy of safety, sanctity and protection. Add the herbs to slowly simmering water and breathe in the newly charged air.

Archangel Protection Rite: Angelica Hex Breaker (Waxing or Full Moon)

Whenever you are going through a hard time or have fears for your family, try this ritual. Angelica, also called the "Heavenly Guardian Flower," is said to first bloom on Archangel Michael's name day. This positive plant is part of the carrot family and is a tall, hollow-stemmed plant with umbrella-shaped clusters of pale white flowers, tinged with green. Candying the stalks in sugar was an old-fashioned favorite, and was also traditionally used to cure colds and relieve coughs. Nowadays, seeds are used to make chartreuse, a digestive and uniquely tasty liqueur. This guardian flower is a protector, as one might expect for a plant associated with archangels, and is used to reverse curses, break hexes and fend off negative energies. Drying and curing the root is a traditional talisman, and it can be carried in your pocket or in an amulet to bring a long life. Many a wise woman has used angelica leaves in baths and spellwork to rid a household of dark spirits. If the bad energy is intense, burn the angelica leaves with frankincense to exorcise them from your space. While you are protecting yourself and your home from negativity during this angelica smudging session, you will also experience heightened psychism. Pay close attention to your dreams after this; important messages will come through.

Cords of Connection: DIY Magical Rope (New Moon is Optimal)

Making this magical tool can be a meditative exercise. Once you have crafted your own magical rope, you should keep it on your altar. This rope binds magic to you, and is ideally made from strands of red wool or ribbon. Nine feet long, it is braided and tied into a loop at one end to represent feminine energy and left loose or frayed at the opposing end to signify the complementary male energy. Crystal beads woven onto the strands of the rope can compound its magical quality. I recommend you use clear quartz crystal beads, which are energy amplifiers, but you can use special stones for various effects: rose quartz for love, citrine for grounding, jade for prosperity and success in work, blue lapis for creativity, and amethyst for improved intuition and psychic ability.

Bottling Up Your Magic (New Moon is Optimal)

In use since medieval times, magic bottles, or spell bottles, can function as protectors of your home. Called witch bottles in the 1600s in England, they were originally used to hold objects for magical uses. They have largely fallen out of use, but you can customize magic bottles for yourself with crystal stoppers for a variety of reasons. You can put one in your garden for healthy plants, on the mantel to protect your home, next to your bed for love and happiness, and in the kitchen for good health. These magic bottles are mostly used for protection, but you can also place into them symbols of your dreams and desires, such as a white rose for peace, the herb rosemary for remembrance, and cinnamon for the spice of life.

For a calm and peaceful home, take a teaspoon of soil from outside your house (or the closest park) and place it into a bottle with some smoky topaz or brown jasper. Place the bottle into the pot of a plant near the entrance of your home. Every time you water the plant, think about the sanctity of your home. As your plant grows, so will the tranquility of your residence.

For luck with money, place three pennies and some pyrite or jade into a bottle and put it on your desk at home or your workplace. Shake the magic jar whenever you think about your finances, and your fortune will improve in three days.

For love, place a pink or red rosebud or rose petal, rose essential oil, and rose quartz into a bottle and keep it at your bedside. Each night, burn a pink candle anointed with the oil from your love-magic bottle. On the seventh day, your prospects for romance will brighten!

Stone Cold Magic: Your Crystal Conjuring Shrine

By building a stone shrine, altar, or power center in your home, you can create a place for daily conjuring, rituals, and thinking. This will set the stage for you to focus your ideas and make them grow. Having a shrine in your home allows you to rid yourself of personal obstacles and invite friendly spirits. Your shrine will spark your inner flame and bring daily renewal. The more use an altar gets, the more energy it builds, making your spells even more effective.

Create your shrine on a low table covered in a white scarf. Set rainbow candles in an arc and then add black and white candles. Place a heatproof bowl containing amber incense (good for creativity and healing), and place it in the center of the rainbow, surrounded by quartz. You should also keep a stick of sage or a seashell on your altar for cleansing the space every day.

Prosperity stones should be placed to the far left on the altar, in the money corner. Romance crystals should sit to the far right on the altar.

The rest of your altar should consist of meaningful, personal symbols. They should reflect your spiritual aspirations. I keep fresh wildflowers in a vase, a statue of a goddess, abalone shells, a magnetite obelisk, and a rock-crystal ball on my altar. An obelisk or pyramid on your altar can be used for writing out desires and wishes. You can use just about anything—photos of loved ones, religious images, and so forth.

With your altar, you can create a bridge between your outer and inner worlds. It can even be a place where you commune with the deepest and most hidden parts of yourself. An altar is where you can honor the rhythms of the season and the rhythms of your own life. An altar is a touchstone, a place to see the sacred and incorporate it into your life each and every day. It can be your special corner of the world where you can rest and connect with your spiritual center. Creating and augmenting your altar every day is one of the most soul-nourishing acts you can do.

Following is a comprehensive overview of different crystals and what their presence on your altar will mean:

Altar Crystal: amazonite, aventurine, carnelian, chrysolite, chrysoprase, citrine, green tourmaline, malachite, yellow fluorite

What They Mean: Creativity

Altar Crystal: amethyst, azurite, celestite, lapis lazuli, moonstone, selenite, smoky quartz, sodalite, star sapphire, yellow calcite

What They Mean: Intuition

Altar Crystal: amethyst, magnetite, rhodochrosite, rose quartz, twinned rock crystals

What They Mean: Love

Altar Crystal: bloodstone, carnelian, citrine, dendritic agate, diamond, garnet, hawk's-eye, moss agate, peridot, ruby, tiger's-eye, topaz, yellow sapphire

What They Mean: Prosperity

Altar Crystal: amber, apache tear, chalcedony, citrine, green calcite, jade, jet, smoky quartz

What They Mean: Protection

Altar Crystal: azurite, chalcedony, chrysocolla, green tourmaline, hematite, rutilated quartz, tiger's-eye

What They Mean: Self-Assurance

Altar Crystal: amber, aventurine, blue jade, dioptase, Herkimer diamond, jasper, kunzite, moonstone, onyx, peridot, quartz, rhodonite

What They Mean: Serenity

Altar Crystal: carnelian, obsidian, quartz, selenite, sodalite, topaz

What They Mean: Success

Altar Crystal: agate, aventurine, bloodstone, calcite, chalcedony, citrine, dioptase, emerald, garnet, orange calcite, ruby, topaz

What They Mean: Vigor

Altar Crystal: emerald, fluorite, Herkimer diamond, moldavite, serpentine, yellow calcite

What They Mean: Wisdom

Witchy Wellness Healing Altar (Waxing Moon is Optimal)

Your altar is your sacred work space, a place imbued with your personal pagan power. I recommend starting with a flat surface, at least two feet across each way for the four directions of the compass. Perhaps you have a favorite antique table, at once simple and ornate. I have set up my altar to face north, long believed to be the origin of primordial energy. North is the direction of midnight, and an altar oriented in this fashion promises potent magic.

Find a pure white square of fabric to drape over your table, just touching the floor. Take two candles in matching holders and place them on the two farthest corners. Place your incense burner exactly in the middle. If you don't have favorite incense yet, start with the ancient essence of frankincense. Select objects that appeal to you symbolically to place on your altar. I have a candlestick of purest amethyst crystal, my birthstone. When I gaze on the candle flame refracted through the beautiful purple gemstone, I feel the fire within me. This inculcates your altar with the magic that lives inside you, that lives inside all of us, and magnifies the ceremonial strength of your workspace. You should decorate your altar until it is utterly and completely pleasing to your eye. After you've been working spells for a bit, an energy field will radiate from your altar.

Fireplace altars today hearken back to this earliest custom. Home and hearth have primal appeal to the comfort of both body and soul. If you have a fireplace, it can become the very heart of your home. The fireplace is also one of the safest places of the ritual work of fire keeping. Sanctify your fireplace with a sprinkling of salt, and then set it up as an altar to the four seasons. Like the Vestal Virgins of old, you can keep a fire burning in a votive glass holder in the back of your fireplace and have an eternal flame. The fireplace can be your simplest altar and a reflection of the work of nature. If you don't have a real fire in your fireplace, you can place in it beautiful sacred objects—pretty rocks, feathers, seashells, glistening crystals, beautiful leaves, and anything representing the holiest aspects of the world around you. Let nature be your guide.

Clearing Energetic Clutter
(Waning Moon is Optimal)

In order to do any healing work, you must clear the clutter that can create blocks. Banish the old, bad energy from your house by following this spell. Make a tea from herb lavender or vervain. Once it cools, dip your finger in the tea and sprinkle it throughout your home while reciting:

Clean and clear, nothing negative near
Only healing and positive energies here.
So mote it be.

Repeat three times, and if you feel the need to clear out any remaining cloud of psychic clutter, add diluted lavender tea water to your cleanser when you wash floors or surfaces. The scent of

calm and clarity will lift the spirits of all who enter your space. The purpose of incense is to release energy into the ritual space, not to create billows of smoke that can cause respiratory problems in the circle. If you or someone else finds incense smoke irritating or worrisome, consider using another symbol of air instead, such as potpourri, fresh flowers, feathers or a fan.

There exist an abundance of incense burners nowadays, so use your discretion and choose one that pleases you—perhaps a smoking dragon or a goddess to hold the fiery embers of your incense would add to the energy of your altar.

Incenses themselves contain inherent energies that you can use to further your intention and promote your purpose. I depend on *Wylundt's Book of Incense,* which I consider to be the ultimate reference for excellent information about essences and properties of incense. It contains an enormous amount of information in regard to loose, cone, stick and cylinder incense. It also tells you how to work with herbs, which part of a plant to use, and how to gather, dry, and store the plants. The following is one of my recipes for an incense to use to cast a circle.

Circle Incense:

- 2 parts myrrh

- 4 parts frankincense

- 2 parts benzoin

- 1 part sandalwood

- 1 part cinnamon

- 1 part rose petals

- 1 part vervain

- 1 part rosemary

- 1 part bay leaf

- 1/2 cup orange peel

This incense will significantly aid the formation of the sphere of energy that is the ritual circle. A fine grind of all the ingredients is the key to good incense, so you should add a mortar and pestle to your list of tools if you intend to make a lot of incense. A blender or food processor is a more modern approach that may save on time and elbow grease, especially if you are making a large batch of incense for a group.

Clearing Incense:

- 1 part sandalwood

- 3 parts myrrh

- 3 parts copal

- 3 parts frankincense

This is an optimal mixture of essences to purify your home or sacred working space. Negative energies are vanquished and the path is cleared for ritual. Open windows and doors when you are burning this clearing incense so the "bad energy" can be released outside. It is also advisable to use this clearing incense if there have been any arguments or other energetic disruptions in your home. You can recreate a sanctuary with this incense.

Dream Incense:

- 2 parts rose petals

- 2 parts cedar

- 1 part camphor

- 1 part lavender

- 6 drops tuberose oil

- 6 drops jasmine oil

This mixture will bring on psychic dreams. If you set up a bedroom altar, place this incense in your censer and allow the scented smoke to imbue your sleeping space with its unique energy before you drift off. Prophetic dreams may come to you and, even better, you will remember them!

Ghostbusting Potion (Waning Moon Optimal)

To rid a house of haunting intrusion, brew a peppermint and clove infusion. Drizzle the potion throughout the space, and out, out, the ghost will race. Burning frankincense and myrrh incense sends negative spirits flying away as well.

Psychic Tuning Fork Meditation – Messages from the Heavens

The great psychic and healer Edgar Cayce used this otherworldly stone azurite for achieving remarkable meditative states, during which he had astoundingly accurate visions and prophetic dreams. Indeed, azurite helps achieve a high state of mental clarity and powers of concentration. If you can't find the answer to a problem in the here and now, try looking for solutions on the astral plane. Write the problem down on paper and place it under a small azurite overnight on a windowsill so it collects moonlight.

At 11:11 a.m., lie comfortably in a quiet and darkened room with the azurite stone placed over your third eye on your forehead. Clear your mind of everything for eleven minutes and meditate. Sit up and listen for the first thing that comes into your mind—it should be the answer, or a message regarding the issue at hand. Write down the words you receive. For the rest of the day you will be in a state of grace and higher mind, during which you will hear information and answers to help guide you in many aspects of your life. If you, like me, enjoy this meditation, you may want to do it every day at 11:11 a.m. and every night at 11:11 p.m. I strongly suggest that you keep a journal of these "azurite answers." You may receive information that you won't understand until many years have passed, making the journal an invaluable resource and key to your very special life.

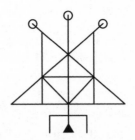

Chapter 3:

North, South, East and West: The Four Directions and Four Elements in Ritual

Each of your days begins with the sun rising in the east and setting in the west. Helios, the great star that enables all life on our manifest planet, rules all your days as the moon rules each night. The following spells can be done in any moon phase as this chapter focuses on the four directions and the elements as used in ritual. The directions all have a specific set of energies you can utilize in your altar and your magical workings:

NORTH - New beginnings, renewal, manifesting

EAST - Initiation, awakening and enlightenment

SOUTH - Emotions and feelings

WEST - Transformation, releasing, the energy of the cloud of darkness

Midnight Moon Purification Ritual

Set up your altar outdoors, weather permitting. The altar should be facing north, the direction associated with the energy of manifestation. North is also the direction of the midnight hour, also known as "The Witching Hour." Find a pure white square of fabric to drape over your altar for clean and clear new beginnings. Take two green candles and place them in green glass holders, and position them in the two farthest corners. Place your censer in between and burn sandalwood, camphor or frankincense for purification. Adorn your altar with objects that connote well-being to you. Perhaps an amethyst candleholder with purple candles, a bowl of bright red apples from your backyard, a dwarf lemon tree bursting with the restorative power of Vitamin C, a cellar of curative salts from the sea. These symbolic items and any others your select will imbue your altar with the magic that lives inside of you and your intention toward good health. It is imperative that it be pleasing to your eye and fills you with gladness when you gaze upon the altar. After you have been performing Midnight Hour rituals for a while, a positive healing energy field will radiate from your altar. Blessed be!

Western Winds of Change Rite

Gather these herbs and stir together into this highly effective clearing incense:

- 1 part sage

- 1 part sandalwood

- 3 parts myrrh

- 3 parts copal

- 3 parts frankincense

This is an optimal mixture of essences to purify your home or sacred working space. Negative energies are vanquished and the path is cleared for ritual. Open windows and doors when you are burning this clearing incense so the "bad energy" can be released outside. It is also advisable to use this clearing incense if there have been any arguments or other energetic disruptions in your home. After a family squabble or, goddess forbid, a break-in, or some incident that makes your office or home or temple space feel violated or less safe, you can dispel the bad with this holy incense.

Sunrise Spell: Blessing Bowl Ritual

While a bowl is not a tool in and of itself, you can utilize bowls in your spellwork often and anytime you are inspired to do so. Three simple ingredients—a red rose, a pink candle and water—can bestow a powerful blessing. The rose signifies beauty, potential, the sunny seasons and love for yourself and others. The candle stands for the element of fire, the yellow flame of the rising sun in the east, harmony, higher intention and the light of the soul. Water represents its own element, flow, the direction of the west, emotions and cleansing. This ritual can be performed alone or with a group in which you pass the bowl around.

Float the rose in a clear bowl of water and light a pink candle beside the bowl. With your left hand, gently stir the water in the bowl and say:

These waters cleanse my soul and being,
Now, with a clear mind and heart, I am seeing,
I am love; my heart is as big as sky and Earth.
From the east to the west, love universal gives life its worth.
Blessings to all, so mote it be.

Keep the blessing bowl on your kitchen altar for three days and three nights. Dry the red rose and keep it on your nightstand or desk where it will always fill your heart with love.

Moonlight and Candles – Earth, Air, Fire Water

The popularity of candles has reached an all-time high. Candles are used by folks from all walks of life, for relaxation, meditation, aromatherapy and, most importantly, to achieve that "peaceful homey" feeling of being in your own sanctuary. This simple yet profound tool can make powerful magic. Take a moment and notice how candlelight transforms a dark room and fills the atmosphere with the energy of magical light. Suddenly the potential for transformation is evident. I don't know about you, but I burn candles 365 days a year! They bring a sense of calm to me, imbuing my personal space with the positive.

Every candle contains all four of the four elements:

Air – Oxygen feeds and fans the candle flame

Earth – Solid wax forms the body of the candle

Water – Melting wax represents the fluid elemental state

Fire – the flame sparks and blazes

How to Charge a Candle

"Charging" a candle means instilling it with magical intent. A candle that has been charged fills your personal space with the intention of all four elements into the celestial sphere. Ritual candles are chosen for their color correspondences and carved, "dressed" or anointed with special oils chosen for their own special energy. Herein is a quick guide to candle color magic:

Black: banishing, absorbing, expelling the negative, healing serious illness

Brown: home, animal wisdom, grounding, physical healing

Dark blue: change, flexibility, the unconscious, psychic powers, emotional healing

Gold: solar magic, money, attraction, the astral plane

Gray: neutrality, impasses, cancellation

Green: money, prosperity, growth, luck, jobs, gardening, youth, beauty, fertility

Light blue: patience, happiness, triumph over depression, calm, deep understanding, compassion

Orange: the law of attraction, success with legal issues, mutability, stimulation, support, encouragement, joy

Pink: love, friendship, kindness, faithfulness, goodness, affection

Purple: female power, stress relief, ambition, healing past wounds, goddesshood, business success

Red: strength, protection, sexuality, vitality, passion, courage, heart, intense feelings of love, good health, power

White: purification, peace, protection from the negative, truth, binding, sincerity, serenity, chastity, gladness, spirit

Yellow: mental power and vision, intelligence, clear thinking, study, self-assurance, prosperity, divination, psychism, abundance, wisdom, power of persuasion, charisma, sound sleep

Once you clarify your intention, cleanse your candles by passing them through the purifying smoke of sage or incense. Further charge your candle by carving a symbol into the wax. You can warm the tip of your ritual knife using a lit match and carve your full intention into the candle wax. As you engrave the appropriate magical words onto the candle, you are charging it with energy and the hope and purpose of your spell. Some highly successful examples of this I have used and witnessed in circle gatherings are: "Healing for my friend who is in the hospital; she will recover for renewed and increased health." "I get the raise I am asking for, and more!" "New true love enters my life in the coming season, blessed be."

Next, you should "dress" your candle with a specific oil. Every essential oil is imbued with a power that comes from plants and flowers of which it is made. You can also use oils to anoint yourself at the crown of the head or at the third eye to increase mental clarity. By using the inherent powers of essential oils, you are increasing and doubling the energies by anointing both your tool—in this case, the candle—and yourself.

Essential oils are highly concentrated extracts of flowers, herbs, root, or resin extract, sometimes dilated in neutral base oil. Try to ensure you are using natural oils instead of manufactured, chemical-filled perfume oil; the synthetics lack any real energy. Also, approach oils with caution, and don't get them in your eyes. Clean cotton gloves are a good idea to keep in your witch's kitchen for handling sensitive materials. You can avoid any mess and protect your magical tools by using oil droppers. Find a trusted herbalist or the wise sage at your local metaphysical shop; usually their years of experience offer much in the way of useful knowledge you can use to your advantage. I have included as much as I can in this at-a-glance guide to oils.

Magical Meanings of Essential Oils:

Astral Projection: jasmine, benzoin, cinnamon, sandalwood

Courage: geranium, black pepper, frankincense

Dispelling negative energy and spirits: basil, clove, copal, frankincense, juniper, myrrh, pine, peppermint, rosemary, Solomon's seal yarrow, vervain

Divination: camphor, orange, clove

Enchantment: ginger, tangerine, amber, apple

Healing: bay, cedar wood, cinnamon, coriander, eucalyptus, juniper, lime, rose, sandalwood, spearmint

Joy: lavender, neroli, bergamot, vanilla

Love: apricot, basil, chamomile, clove, copal, coriander, rose, geranium, jasmine, lemon, lime, neroli, rosemary, ylang-ylang

Luck: orange, nutmeg, rose, vervain

Peace: lavender, chamomile

Prosperity: basil, clove, ginger, cinnamon, nutmeg, orange, oak, moss, patchouli, peppermint, pine, aloe

Protection: bay, anise, black pepper, cedar, clove, cypress, copal, eucalyptus, frankincense, rose geranium, lime, myrrh, lavender, juniper, sandalwood, vetiver

Sexuality: Cardamom, lemongrass, amber, rose, clove, olive, patchouli

Inner-Serenity Spell

For inner peace, take a walk in the woods, a stroll on the beach, or just relax in your backyard. Bring a stick, seven leaves from an ash or oak tree, several stones, and matches. With the stick, draw a circle on the ground and mark four directions: north, east, south and west.

Place the stones at the center of the circle. Concentrate upon your connection to the earth and how to honor that in your life. Say:

Good luck rises for me in the East;
My music rises in the South;
My wishes rise in the West;
From the North, my dreams will come true.

Earth, Air, Fire, Water – Ritual Tool Sanctification

You should design a personal consecration ritual for your magical tools. Use the following ritual as a simple "temple template" to build on. In essence, in this ritual you are dedicating yourself and your tools for the betterment of all and setting a foundational intention for your good works. Every time you acquire a new tool or treasure, perform this rite. As you grow in experience, you can embellish the ritual. Refer to your own Book of Shadows. Is there a certain phase of the moon that brings you more clarity? Should you use corresponding colors, crystals, essential oils, incenses, and herbs for your own astrological sun and moon sign? Is there a specific deity with whom you feel an affinity? Use these correspondences to begin designing the rituals of your dreams. The more associations you learn and use, the more effective your power will grow. Keep good notes of your ritual work in your Book of Shadows, and soon you will become a "maestro of magic."

Power Up: Ritual Tools That Need Charging

You will need a symbol of each of the four elements—air, earth, fire, and water—such as: a candle for fire, incense for air, a cup or water, a bowl of salt.

One was to design your own ritual is to work with the four elements. Choose a symbol from the information here. Also let your instinct guide you to choose as you wish or what you are inspired by.

Take the new ritual tool and pass it through the scented smoke of the incense and say:

Now inspired with the breath of air.

Then pass the tool swiftly through the flame of the candle and say:

Burnished by fire.

Sprinkle the tool with water and say:

Purified by water.

Dip the tool into the bowl of salt and say:

Empowered by the earth.

Hold the tool before you with both hands and imagine an enveloping, warm white light purifying the tool. Now say:

Steeped in spirit and bright with light.

Place the cleansed tool upon your altar and say:

By craft made and by craft charged and changed, this tool [fill in the actual name: boline, Book of Shadows, etc.] *I will use for the purpose of good in this world and in the realm of the gods and goddesses. I hereby consecrate this tool _____.*

Other tools you will use in ritual are more intangible. These include your breath, your intuition, your psychic powers, and your ability to focus your mental powers and spiritual intentions. Because they are intangible, only your intention can purify them. From time to time, you will use colors, herbs, oils, crystals, and numbers. Many of these ritual correspondences and associations have been passed down through the centuries, whereas many of them were invented by modern authors. Information on them can be found in the appendices.

Crystals can also be charged. However, tools that come from nature and are not "manmade," but are of divine design, such as flowers, feathers, and herbs, already contain an intrinsic magic of their own and can be used as you find them.

Your tools will collect and hold the magic that lives inside you. They will become instilled with your energy and stored at your altar or in your sacred space. They will become your power source and will magnify the strength of your ritual work. Your altar should be a place of peace and meditation where your spirit can soar. Adorned with your treasured objects and the tools of your practice, it is a place of focus where you can enrich your life through ritual. You can create a wellspring of spirit so you can live an enchanted life every single day.

You can also perform rituals and make magic without any tools or implements at all. Your intention alone is extremely powerful. This simple approach could be called "zen magic." When you perform ritual in this way, you are one step closer to the methods by which early men and women created ceremonies.

Intention Magic: Consecration Candle Spell

Write your intention on paper and then speak aloud:

*Thus I consecrate this candle in the name of [your favorite deity].
So this flame will burn brightly and light my way with the element
of fire.*

Place the anointed candle in the candleholder, light it, and say:

Blessed candle, light of the Goddess,
I burn this light of [deity's name].
Hear my prayer, O, [name the deity], hear my need.
Grant my wish and give me hope.
Do so with all your grace,
And magical speed.

Now read your intention as you wrote it on the paper. Roll the paper into a scroll and, using a few drops of the warm wax from your intention candle, seal your sacred statement. Place the paper on your altar or in a special place where it can be safe until your intention is realized.

Powers of the East, West, North and South Sanctuary Spell (Waning Moon, New Moon)

Every kitchen has a box of salt. This most common of seasonings is essential to physical health and also the health of your home. With a bowl of salt alone, you can purify your home every day and have a "safe zone" for ritual work. You can leave a bowl of pure salt in any room you feel is in need of freshening; the salt absorbs negativity. Many a witch uses this homely approach on a daily basis early in the day, tidying up and cleansing energy to charge a home with positivity.

In your kitchen, take a bowl of water, freshly drawn and a small cup of salt. Take the vessel of water and sprinkle in as much as you feel is needed. Anoint your fingers by dipping them in the salt water and then around your third eye in the middle of your forehead.

Now turn to the east and say:

Power of the East,
Source of the Sun rising,
Bring me new beginnings.

After speaking, sprinkle some of the water in the eastern part of your kitchen.

Face south and say:

Source of the Starry Cross,
Place of warmth and light,
Bring me joy and bounty.

Scatter droplets of salt water in the southern direction.

Face the west and speak aloud:

Powers of the West,
Source of oceans, mountains, and deserts all,
Bring me the security of the ground beneath my feet.

Scatter droplets of water in the west side of your kitchen.

Face north now and speak aloud:

Powers of the North,
Bringer of winds and the polestar.
Show me vision and insight.

Sprinkle water in the northern area of the room.

End this ritual by sprinkling water and salt all around your home, especially around windows, sills, doorways and thresholds where energy passes in and out as visitors and delivery people come and go. In this way, you are cleansing and managing the energy of your space. After a distressing occurrence, you can repeat this ritual and then leave a bowl of salt out for 24 hours so it can rid your sacred space of negative "vibes."

Lady of Silver Magic: Full-Moon Circle Gathering

The full moon is the most powerful time of the month and the perfect time to celebrate with special people in your life. This ritual will heighten your spirituality, your friendships, and your connection to the powers of the universe.

As I write this, it is a full moon in Pisces, and I look forward to getting together with some of the sisterhood, some fellow spiritual seekers, and kicking up our heels in celebration of life and asking for what we need from the universe. We will wait until midnight, the traditional witching hour. We will gather in one of our favorite spots near water under the magical moonlight.

Here is our recipe for ritual: We place the biggest crystal we can—usually a geode, an amethyst chunk, or a big quartz or rock crystal—in the middle of the altar. We place a goblet of wine before an image of the Goddess. We all bring candles in sturdy, tempered-glass votives to light our way, and we perform a rite we learned from our elders. Each of us holds a crystal that is our touchstone.

You can perform this ritual in your home or garden or a sacred place of your choosing. Designate a leader who will perform all the incantations as the group forms a circle. Begin with the appropriate chanting:

Oh, lady of silver magic, we honor you here,
In this place, sacred and safe.
This circle is in your honor.

The person in the northern point of the circle places her candle and her crystal on the ground as the leader chants:

Blessed one, all earth is yours.
May we all heal,
May we all draw strength,
May we grow.

The person in the eastern point places her candle and her crystal on the ground while the leader chants:

Oh, lady of laughter and joy, so is the sky yours, too.
May the air be clear and pure,
And the clouds sweet with wind and rain.

The person at the southern point lays down her crystal and candle while the chanter speaks:

Oh, lady of summer, each season is yours.
May each spring bring flowers and crops for all.

The person at the western point lays down her candle and crystal while the chanter speaks:

Goddess of the waters,
The rivers and the ocean are yours.
May they once more flow crystal clear.
Lady, we have built this circle in your honor.
Be with us here now.

Now each member of the circle goes to the altar and kneels, placing her candle and crystal on the altar. Each takes a sip from the goblet of wine and says:

I toast thee, bright lady,
In your honor. Blessed be.

Then, all members pick up rattles and drums and sing and dance under the sparkling crystals in the sky. If you are able to observe every full moon with a ritual gathering, your life will be very rich, indeed.

West With the Night –A Setting Sun Spell (All Lunar Phases)

To clear energy and prepare for a week of calm clarity, find your favorite white flower—iris, lily, rose, one that is truly beautiful to your eye. Monday's setting sun is the time for this spell, immediately after the sun goes below the horizon. Anoint a white candle with clary sage oil and place on your altar. Take your single white blossom and add that to your altar in a bowl of freshly drawn water. Place sage leaves on a glass dish in front of the lit candle and speak aloud:

This fire is pure; this flower is holy, this water is clear.
These elements purify me.
I walk in light with nothing in my way.
My energy is pure, my spirit is holy, my being is clear.
White light burns bright in me and all the words I say.
So mote it be. And so it is.

Burn the sage in the fire of the candle and put in the glass dish where is can turn into ash, smudging as it burns. Stand in front of your altar and breathe in slowly and deeply six times. On the last strongest exhalation, blow the candle out.

Middle Earth Magic: How to Use a Crystal Ball

Crystal balls have their own authority and they can strongly influence the development of our psychic abilities. You should think of the crystal as a container that houses your energy. Make sure it feels right for you. The crystal should feel comfortable to hold—not too heavy and not too light. You should not allow anyone else to touch your crystal ball. If someone does touch it, place the ball in a bowl of sea salt overnight to cleanse it of outside energy and influence. Because quartz crystal balls have an inherent power, you have to practice working with them first. Pure quartz crystal balls can be quite expensive, but the price is worthwhile if you are serious about harnessing your intuition and using it for good. Don't expect your experiences to be like the movies. Most of the people I know who use crystal balls, including many healers and teachers, see cloudy and smoky images.

Work with a partner to sharpen your psychic skills. Sit directly across from your partner with the crystal ball between you. Close your eyes halfway and look *at* the ball and *into* the ball while harnessing your entire mind. Empty out all other thoughts and focus as hard as you can. You will sense your third eye, the traditional seat of psychic awareness, begin to open and project into the crystal ball. By practicing this way, you will train your mind. The patterns you see will become clearer and your impressions more definite. You should trust that what you are seeing is real. Find a place of knowing, as I do with my stomach. Verbalize to your partner what you see, and then listen to your partner as she reveals her visions to you. After at least three rounds of individual reading and revealing, share visions at the same time to learn whether you are seeing the same things!

You should also do crystal ball meditations on your own. In a darkened room, sit and hold your crystal ball in the palms of both hands. Touch it to your heart and then gently touch it to the center of your forehead, where your third eye is located. Then hold the ball in front of your physical eyes and, sitting very still, gaze into it for at least three minutes. Envision pure white light in the ball and hold on to that image. Practice the white-light visualization for up to a half hour and then rest your mind, your eyes and your crystal ball. If you do this every day, within a month you should start to become an adept at crystal ball gazing.

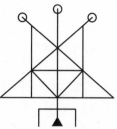

Chapter 4:

Everyday Spells: Harnessing the Power of the Moon for Your Magic

S ometimes, you just can't wait for the next full moon to make some magic; you need to take action today with tried and true spellwork that really works. Maybe you have unexpected bills and need more money, or maybe you spotted an intriguing stranger whilst in line for your morning latte. Perhaps you have need of wisdom from above, or you feel down in the dumps. No matter what you are looking for, here is a set of every day spells for almost every basic need in life—even help finding parking!

Magic on the Move – Parking Pendant (All Moon Phases)

Hang a red jasper crystal attached to a string on your rearview mirror in your car and your parking problems will soon be over. When you need a spot, touch the jasper and say, "See the parking spot; be the parking spot." Remember to always give thanks to the parking gods and goddesses to remain in their favor.

Privacy Magic: Banish Space Invaders

Is your office mate overly interested in your conversations with your mom? Do you have nosy neighbors or a nightmare roommate? Combat other people's cluelessness with crystals! If you have problems with the people next door, place jet at your door or bury it by the fence. If you have an intrusive housemate or guest, place jet on the mantle or bookshelves and wear jet jewelry to take back your personal space straightaway. This is a wonderfully respectful and peacekeeping way to honor your need for solitude that harms no one. Use this spell anytime you need protection from "space invaders." Nosy people are often lonely so, when the time is right, offer a cup of tea and a chat and you will be doubtless rewarded for your largesse tenfold. Kindness is a very powerful magic.

Ritual Knotting – Cords to Strengthen Your Life's Energy (New Moon is Optimal)

All you need is a paper scroll and a length of red thread or cord. The color red signifies life and active energy. After you feel you have fully focused your energy into the scroll, roll it up.

Now, proceed to tie knots in the order of the following traditional chant:

By knot of one, this ritual is begun.
By knot of two, my wish comes true.
By knot of three, so mote it be.
By knot of four, the magic is even more.

By knot of five, the gods are alive.
By knot of six, my intention is fixed.
By knot of seven, under the influence of heaven.
By knot of eight, I change my fate.
By knot of nine, all powers are divine.

When you have completed the knots, tie the cord around your scroll. Note in your Book of Shadows when the power of this spell unfolds. This will be very useful for future knotting work.

Friendly Feasts: Rite of Connection

Before you enjoy a friendly repast together, hold hands and recite:

Sister, brother, tribe of the soul, ones who care.
Merry may we meet again to share.
Breaking bread and quaffing mead
We draw closer in word and deed.
Blessing of love to all!

Inspiration Infusion: Spell in a Cup

Your morning pot of tea can be a daily ritual you use according to your needs. If, upon rising, you feel a bit blue, brew up some bergamot. As you sip the soothing libration, you will feel your spirits lift and you can greet the day stronger and infused with this simple and true magic. Along with healing and energizing properties, herbal teas can aid the mind. Try the following blends:

- Bergamot dissipates negativity and uplifts.

- Basil lends a sense of serenity.

- Rosemary supports physical well-being.

- Orange creates sheer joy.

Grounding Meditation

Because the world we live in today is very much about getting in your head and staying there, many of us have to make a concentrated effort to become grounded and in touch with our bodies and with the natural world around us.

Grounding is the technique for centering yourself within your being, getting into your body and out of your head. Grounding is the way to reconnect and balance yourself through the power of the element of earth. When you see someone walking past talking on their cell phone, you know that they are not grounded.

Service to Mother Earth: A Walking Meditation

As you walk, take the time to look and really see what is in your path. For example, my friend Brenda takes a bag with her and picks up every piece of garbage in her path. She does this as an act of love for the earth. During the ten years I have known her, she has probably turned a mountain of garbage into recycled glass, paper and plastic. Goddess bless!

Rock Your World: Talismanic Stones for Success

These stones pave the path to prosperity for everyone. Use them on your altar, piled up on an arrangement on your desk at work or keep them in your pocket. This earth-based energy acts like a battery to boost you along.

Azurite strengthens mental powers.

Chalcedony gives you get-up-and-go!

Emerald aids in problem solving.

Opal encourages faithful service.

Pearl engenders material wealth.

Quartz helps overcome fear of rejection.

Sapphire helps with goal setting.

Tourmaline promotes an attitude of accomplishment.

Rose-Colored Glass: Energy Boosters

If you want to jump-start your life and bring about positive change, tap into the power of the rose and red stones. Stones of this color spectrum contain life's energy and can help you become more motivated, energetic and vibrant. Wear this list of rosy and red stones or place them on your desk and throughout your home for an instant boost: alexandrite, carnelian, garnet, red coral, red jasper, rhyolite, rose jasper, and ruby. The new moon phase is an

excellent time to introduce this vibrancy into your life, but you should also rock them anytime you need a boost.

The World's Easiest Love Potion

Elixirs are very simple potions made by placing a crystal or gemstone in a glass of water for at least seven hours. Remove the stone and drink the crystallized water. The water will now carry the vibrational energy of the stone, the very essence of the crystal.

Place into a glass of water:

- *Carnelian*

- *garnet*

- *rough ruby*

- *red coral*

- *red jade*

- *jasper*

- *red sardonyx*

- *cuprite*

- *aventurine*

- *red calcite*

Mix and match and remember, if you only have access to a rough ruby and a tiny chunk of jasper, so be it—that is still a lot of love in a jar!

Place the elixir in the love corner of your room or on your altar. Light amber incense and a red candle and speak aloud:

This jade is my joy, the garnet of my grace.

Leave the water on your altar for seven hours or overnight and drink it upon awakening. Your life energy will quicken and you should feel very upbeat and good to go. Share the love!

Wands are Wonderful: Be a Crafty Conjurer

Gandalf, Glinda and Harry Potter shouldn't have all the fun. It is a marvelous thing to make your own wand. Start with a tree branch that has fallen to the ground on its own. Sand and polish the rough edges, as it is a wand and not a weapon. Then give it a good smudging. Hot-glue on a large quartz crystal onto the wand near the handle, and hot-glue on any crystals featuring properties that will complement your magic.

Moonstone Mirror Magic (Full Moon is Optimal)

Moonstone is a psychic mirror, especially for females. Wise women of ancient India were the first to figure this out. If you are feeling out-of-sorts or off-center, turn to this lovely stone, sacred to the shining orb in our night sky. Under moonlight, gaze first at the moon and then at your smooth, round moonstone and look for the answer to your personal mystery. A message will come to you in the form of a dream this night. Keep a journal at your bedside to record this moonlit message.

Time Is On Your Side Spell

A gift of a clock is lucky. Luckier still is to hear two clocks chiming together at a happy moment. If you are kissing, happy in company, meeting someone you like, concluding a business deal or launching a project, or indeed, in the midst of any other hopeful occasion, and you hear two clocks striking together, link fingers with the other person, or kiss them on the cheek.

Say aloud:

Two clocks have struck,
'Tis set for luck.

Take careful note of the hour.

For the next two days, observe the hour again and think of the event that has just taken place; wish hard for luck on that matter once again. Good luck will surely attend you—whatever the matter on hand concerns.

Make a Wish Upon the Wind: A Happiness Ritual

Bluebirds are so famous they have given their name to the bluebird of happiness. The robin has been associated with the same signs of cheerfulness and joy. Seeing a bluebird or robin, you should immediately make a wish: it must be something unselfish, and not dependent on anyone else. As the bird flies off, set your wish ascending. Wish hard for steadily increasing happiness and release from strains. Whether a bluebird or a robin, if you see the bird again with a few days in exactly the same place, your wish will certainly be granted.

Here are some more magical wings and prayers:

Crow feathers: These indicate loss and mourning. Try not to be frightened but look at them as indicators of the cycles of life, death, and rebirth.

Hummingbird feathers: These bring joy, beauty, and bliss. Take time out to have a good time and to share with the people you love.

Swan feathers: These are the sign of grace. As swans mate for life, a swan feather can also mean a soul mate or good relationship is on the horizon.

Yellowhammer feathers: These are the symbol for hearth and home. Seeing a yellowhammer feather in your path means you will have a happy new home.

Magpie feathers: These are just plain good medicine for any kind of illness. Magpies bring purification.

Put a Cork In It – Charmed Life Charm

The next time you enjoy a beverage sealed with a cork, keep the cork. This does not have to be a champagne cork—they are all lucky. When a bottle is shared and the occasion is a happy event or joyous moment, secret away the cork from the bottle, making a wish for repetition of the pleasure as you do so, and placing a coin in a slit in the top of the cork.

Now you must sleep on the cork every night (under your pillow) and keep it in your pocket all the next day. Rub the cork any day thereafter when you wish to hear from the other person or people who shared the bottle with you; do not wish for love but rather for continuing happiness. The cork symbolizes buoyancy, not love.

Celebrate these events throughout the year to find your lucky cork:

January 1: New Year's Day

February 14: St. Valentine's Day

March 8: International Women's Day

April 22: Earth Day

May 1: May Day, Beltane

June 19: Juneteenth

July 20: National Moon Day

August 4: Dom Pérignon invents champagne in 1693—celebrate!

September 20: International Day of Peace

October 15: Festival of Mars (Ancient Rome)

November 5: Guy Fawkes Day

December 5: International Volunteers Day

Sylvan Spell: Planting Magic

This is a lovely spell to do if you are given a small tree as a gift, to wish for strength and good health for you and your love. Before you plant the sapling, tie a bow in some colored ribbon, and plant the bow with a small heart symbol in the soil under the roots of the tree. After you have planted the tree, water it well—especially with one or two tears of love, if possible! Make a wish that both you and your love will grow strong and enduring as the tree takes root and begins to flourish. When the tree bears its first leaf, press it in a book associated with the one you love. As long as you tend your tree with love, you will both enjoy blooming health and vitality.

Conjuring Clairvoyance: Open Your Third Eye

Saffron water is made by boiling one teaspoon of saffron in two cups of distilled water. Dip your hands in the water, touch your "third eye" at the center of your forehead and speak aloud:

Ishtar, Athena, Diana, Astarte – fill me with your presence.
This night, I am whole. I am at peace.
With each breath, you do inspire.
So mote it be.

Henceforth, you will understand things more clearly and have foresight. This is a muscle which can be developed with more use. Practice and you'll find you have advance notice of what is to come.

Inspiration Infusion: Enhance Your Mental Powers

I recommend growing a pot of hardy sage so you can always clear energy and increase your psychic potential. Another useful herb is mint, which comes from the Latin *mentha*, and literally means "thought." It is called the flower of eternal refreshment. Woven into a crown, it bestows brilliance, artistic inspiration and prophetic ability. Burned, it is especially potent.

Here is a wonderfully simple tool for awakening the mind and attuning to the high powers. Take dried mint stalks and dried sage in equal parts and roll together into a wand. Bind with multi-colored string, and before any ritual, tarot reading, or spellcrafting, "smudge" your house with the wand by lighting the leafy end and passing the smoke around. This will purify your space.

Become An Alchemist: Lunar Libation

No matter what sign or moon phase, witch's brews can improve your life. Tea conjures a very powerful alchemy because when you drink it, you take the magic inside. For an ambrosial brew with the power to calm any storm, add a sliver of ginger root and a pinch each of chamomile and peppermint to a cup of hot black tea. Before you drink, pray:

This day I pray for calm, for health,
And the wisdom to see the beauty of each waking moment.
Blessings abound.
So mote it be.

Herbal teas can also nourish the soul and heal the body:

Blueberry leaf tea reduces mood swings, evens glucose levels, and helps varicose veins.

Nettle raises energy levels, boosts the immune system, and is packed with iron and vitamins.

Fennel awakens and uplifts, freshens the breath, and aids colon health.

Echinacea lends an increased and consistent sense of well-being, and prevents colds and flu.

Ginger root calms and cheers while aiding digestion, nausea and circulation.

Dandelion root grounds and centers, provides many minerals and nutrients, and cleanses the liver of toxins.

Mood Magic: Blue Moon Balm

For a dreary day and a dark mood, use the strength of the olden unguent to release both mind and body. This desert plant produces a protective oil, which works as both a sunscreen and a moisturizer. Combine the following oils with either four ounces of unscented body lotion, or two ounces of olive oil or sweet almond oil:

- *2 drops chamomile oil*

- *2 drops neroli*

- *8 drops aloe*

- *6 drops rose oil*

Shake the oils together and place in a corked pottery jar. Sit quietly in a room lit only by one blue candle, and rub the balm gently into your skin after a bath. Pray aloud:

Work thy spell to heal and nurse.
Blessed balm, banish my pain.
Harm to none and health to all.

Sweet Dreams: Do It Yourself House Magic

Tranquil sleep and pleasant, illuminating dreams are the surest sign you have achieved peace of mind. An enchantment pillow will ensure you experience your fair share of nocturnal reverie and wake up refreshed. Take a pink satin pillowcase and stuff it with well-mixed dried rose petals, chamomile, mint and woolly thyme. Sew it with purple thread and, before the final stitch, whisper:

I call upon the powers of the Night to watch over me,
To hear my heart's desires and bring me what my soul requires.
Blessings to one and all.

Knot the final stitch three times, place the pillow inside your pillowcase, and kiss the pillow. If you have been having problems sleeping, that will end this night.

Light Your Own Fire: Sage Wisdom (New Moon is Optimal)

Every witch should grow a pot of sage or a big patch in a garden. Sage is a must-have on hand for clearing energy. It also increases psychic potential. Most pagans are highly imaginative and very inventive folk. Whether your passion is growing an artful garden, throwing pots, cookery or music, you can stay in better touch with your personal muse. Call her to you anytime, day or night, by your own design. This is especially important if you are feeling uninspired or struggling with a bout of writer's block.

Head out to your garden or the sunny spot on the deck where your hardiest sage grows. Take three large and extra long sticks of your favorite incense and bind strands of sage around the incense with purple thread. Tie it off and you have a sage wand. Before any creative endeavor, you can light this wand and wave it around your workspace, filling the area with inspiration. Close your eyes and meditate upon the work you will begin. You have cleared your space and invited the muse; your work will be superb, worthy of notice from the gods and goddesses.

Dark Moon Magic: Symbol Writing

If you wish to make direct contact with your subconscious, here is a way to see through the veil between two worlds and enter the recesses of your mind. At any herbal store or metaphysical shop, obtain dried mugwort, dried patchouli or wormwood. The latter is a bit harder to come by, but worth the try.

Crumble any one of these herbs between your hands until it is gently ground into an almost-powdery consistency. Pour the herb into a baking pan. Make sure the crumbled herb dust is evenly spread over the surface of the pan.

Light yellow candles and close your eyes. Take the forefinger of your left hand and touch the center of the pan. Run your finger back and forth in a completely random pattern—don't think, just rely on your instincts for two minutes. Open your eyes, look at the pattern you have drawn, and write down what the symbols and designs bring to mind. Also write down the thoughts you were having while you were drawing. This ritual is best performed in the new moon phase, but if you have an urgent need to connect with your innermost self, you can do it anytime in the darkest of the night.

Truth-Seeking Spell

If you find yourself in need of help resolving a problem or uncovering new resources within yourself, try the following tried and true rite. Take a piece of plain white paper and a blue pen and have it at the ready.

On a Thursday, light some blue candles and chant the following affirmation:

Fears and doubt, begone from me!
I have the courage to break free.
I have the wisdom to know and the strength to grow.
I call upon my inner guide to hear and see my truth.

Repeat this four times while the candle burns. Embrace your intuition and trust it with all your heart. Now write down what comes into your mind with the blue pen. You may even feel tingling at the top of your head, which is a very good sign. Knowing the truth can sometimes be uncomfortable, but it is important as a guide for your life.

Ready, Set, Go Spell

On a Monday, or any day you need to ready yourself for important events, meetings, or anything high-pressure, set aside a half-hour of quiet time and brew up some willpower to help you in any creative endeavors. Light a white candle anointed with peppermint oil and light spicy incense (cinnamon works well, if you can get it).

Take a sprig of mint, warm milk, and cinnamon sticks and stir together clockwise in a white mug. Say aloud:

Herb of minthe and spicy mead,
Today is the day I shall succeed
In every word and every deed.
So mote it be.

Quaff the cup and "sit for a spell," eyes closed, envisioning your new horizons. Keep the cinnamon sticks on your altar as a symbol of the power of encouraging words.

Eye Enchantment: Rite of Twilight

For most of us, the minute we open our eyes the day begins, and we put them to work for our jobs, self-care, housework and even Facetiming loved ones and Skyping business associates. If you are a designer or artist of any sort, you most likely use your eyes to create, so caring for them is essential. Take two small muslin bags and three ounces of dried chamomile flowers. Divide the herb in half, stuff the bags, and sew them shut.

Place the eye bags in a bowl and pour a quarter cup of boiling water over them. Cover them and let sit for a half-hour. Squeeze the excess water out of the bags and place over your eyes. Your eyes and your artistic vision should both be rejuvenated quickly. This healing rite is best performed at twilight but, anytime your peepers need some "TLC," steep away.

Cauldron of Fire Ritual

Here is a wonderful way friends can help each other get rid of fears, creative blocks, and the shrill voice of the inner critic. Ideally, this spell is done during the waning moon or on November 1 or December 31—the witchy holidays when the veil between worlds is believed to be thinnest.

Get a metal kettle and an outdoor firepot or little grill, and for each of the friends you have invited, a pen and two pieces of paper. Sit around the fire, relax, and talk about what challenges you face in attaining your artistic goals. Write on a piece of paper what comes up for you. Go around the circle and read from your list of blocks. Then, with great intention, place each paper on the fire. After everyone is done, silently meditate, and write your hope for the future. Now, reversing the order of speaking, go around the circle and share your dreams. Fold the paper and carry it with you in your purse or wallet. Your vision for the future will take on a life of its own.

Dis-Spelling All Fear: Full Moon Rite

For overcoming panic, anxiety or your innermost fears, you can turn to your banishing block touchstone. You probably already have a crystal you turn to, but if not, allow me to recommend the rose-red marvel known as Rhodochrosite. This striking stone is also invaluable for overcoming fear and paranoia (mental unease). Rhodochrosite abets a more positive worldview. One of the simplest and best aspects of this crystal is that it will help you to sleep more peacefully, shoving apprehension, worry, and woe out of your mind so you can heal body and soul. Your dreams will be positive, too. This is a remarkable stone for affirming the self, allowing for absolute self-acceptance and self-forgiveness. Rhodochrosite brings together the spiritual plane and the material place. This crystal is important because it permits the heart to feel hurt and pain deeply, and this processing of emotions nurtures growth.

Sit on the floor, legs crossed, and breathe deeply nine times. Take the touchstone into your hands and chant:

That which came from the sky, enter into me.
As was the moon full, so am I now.
And so I go, with this light, full and bright.
So mote it be.

Repeat this at least six times, until you feel the energy of the stone passing into you. Now, go conquer!

Count Your Blessings: Morning Moon Meditation

Plan this for an early morning when you can still see a sliver of the moon as the sun rises. Sit in a comfortable position in front of your altar and meditate. Think about your blessings. What are you grateful for at this moment? There is a powerful magic in recognizing all that you possess. Breathe steadily and deeply, inhaling and exhaling slowly for twenty minutes. Then chant:

Great Goddess, giver of all the fruits of this earth,
Of all bounty, beauty, and well-being,
Bless all who give and receive these gifts.
I am made of sacred earth, purest water,
Sacred fire, and wildest wind.
Blessings upon me. Blessings upon thee,
Mother Earth and Sister Sky.
So mote it be.

A wonderful practice is to record your gratitudes in your Book of Shadows or a thankfulness journal. At the end of the lunar year, you'll have your own Book of Blessings you can reflect upon and share with others.

Moon Cakes and Ale: Full Moon Festival

Here is a pagan ritual I have performed on weekends, when the full moon shines bright. Over the years, I have added many embellishments, such as astrological or holiday themes. This basic ritual, Moon Cakes and Ale, however, is a timeless and powerful classic.

Gather a group of friends either outdoors under the moon or in a room large enough for dancing, drumming, and singing. Have the guests bring a cake of their choice as well as a cider, mead, beer or juice to share. Place the offerings in the center, on an altar table. Then light a sage leaf and green and brown candles for home and hearth.

Once everyone is seated, the host or designated leader intones:

Gods of nature, bless these cakes,
That we may never suffer hunger.
Goddess of the Harvest, bless this ale,
That we may never go without drink.

The eldest and the youngest of the circle rise and serve the food and drink to everyone in the circle. Last, they serve each other. The ritual leader pronounces the blessing again. Then everyone says together, "Blessed be."

The feasting begins, ideally followed by a lot more ale and lively dancing. A wonderful way to keep a group of friends connected is for a different person to host the circle one Saturday each month.

Exorcise Your Demons: Community Healing Gathering

Here is an ancient way of casting out demons and bringing new tidings for your friendships and family. Buy a big bag of dried beans and invite all your friends over. In ancient times, many pagan people—from the Greeks to the Incan Indians—believed that beans contained evil spirits.

Ideally performed during an eclipse when that which is hidden is revealed, procure bags of beans and invite your tribe over. Go to your roof, a hill, or wherever you can "get high." Give everyone a handful of beans and start throwing them down one at a time, with each toss calling out whatever you want to kiss goodbye—a job, a bad relationship, whatever your personal demons may be. After you have discarded all the discord from your life, you and your friends can celebrate the lifting of your burdens.

Lucky Charms and Ring of Power: A Protection Spell

Most people don't realize that the classic charm bracelet is decorated with magical symbols representing the wearer's wishes. For wealth, wear a Roman coin on your bracelet; for love, try a heart. For protection, a pure silver ring worn on the right pinkie has the greatest magical power, especially when engraved with your birth sign or astrological glyph and the sacred pentagram. To instill the ring with protective power, clasp it over your heart and call out:

Ring of power, shield and encircle me.
By your charm, I am free.

Blessed be me. All are one.
Blessings to all and harm to none.

Vision Quest: New Moon Conjuring Incense

You can access your prophetic capabilities with a Wednesday incense ritual using:

- 3 palmfuls ground chicory root

- 1 palmful ground cloves

- 3 palmfuls cinquefoil*

Cinquefoil is in the dandelion family. If you can't find any, substitute dried fern fronds or dandelions from your front yard.

Mix and burn the herbs in your fireplace in an outside sanctuary spot or on your altar while concentrating on a question. Maybe you are considering a new home, or whether to take a new job or pursue a business venture. Use this time to cleanse your mind of all concerns, worries and thoughts, making way for pure insight. Answers will come.

Treasure Hunting Tea: A Medieval Charm

The humble dandelion, oft abhorred by lawn keepers, hides its might well. Dandelion root tea can call upon the spirit of anyone whose advice you might need. Simply place the brew on your nightstand and say the spirit's name seven times; he or she will visit your dreams and answer your questions. In Chaucer's day, this method was used to find lost treasures.

A Happy (and Hoppy) Household Blessing

When you or a friend move into a new home, place a wreath or bundle of dried hops and eucalyptus on the front door. Walk through the door, light your favorite incense and a brown candle, and lie down in the center of the front room. Whisper:

House of my body, I accept your shelter.
House of my spirit, I receive your blessings.
Home to my heart, I am open to joy.
And so it is. And so it shall be.

Gloom Away: Lunar Levity

I don't know about you, but I occasionally wake up on the wrong side of the bed. The best way to avoid that is to brew up this lovely aromatic spray and use it to scent your bedroom before you retire. When your linens and personal space smell sweet, your dreams are guaranteed to be the same. This custom recipe works wonders on you or anyone in your environment who might need a lift. Combine the following essential oils:

- *two drops peppermint*

- *two drops bergamot*

- *two drops lavender*

- *four drops rose*

- *four drops neroli*

Add the mixture to a quart of distilled water, and spray the air while chanting:

Gloom and doom be gone.
Welcome, sweet spirits, into this house,
With harm to none. So mote it be.

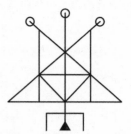

Chapter 5:

Your Magical Week: Solar Days and Lunar Nights

Each day of the week has specific correspondences and meanings. Here is an at-a-glance guide to the days of the week, gleaned from the mythologies of centuries put to practice for different types of ritual. I do a money-enhancing ritual every Thursday, or "Thor's Day," which is the day for prosperity. Perhaps you want new love in your life; if so, try a "Freya's Day" ritual on a Friday night.

Sunday is the day for healing and vitality, as well as creativity and new hope. The colors for this day are gold, orange and yellow, and the sacred stones for this day are also in those colors: amber, citrine, carnelian, and topaz. Sunday's herbs and incense are cloves, cedar, chamomile, frankincense, amber, sunflower and heliotrope.

Monday, or "Moon Day," is a dreamy day for intuition, beauty, women's rituals and your home. The colors are shiny silvers; pearl, pale rose, white and lavender, reflective like the moon. The gems and stones are similarly shaded moonstone, pearl, quartz crystal, fluorite and aquamarine. The herbs and incense are night blooming jasmine, myrtle, moonwort, vervain, white rose, poppy and camphor.

Tuesday is the day for action. "Mars's Day" is the time for high energy in your career, for physical activity, for aggression in meetings, and for strong sensuality. Red is the day's color, and the corresponding gems and crystals are ruby, garnet, carnelian, bloodstone and pink tourmaline. Incense and herbs for Mars's Day are red roses, pine, carnation, nettle, patchouli, pepper and garlic.

Wednesday, or "Odin's Day," is when the planets of communication, Mercury and Chiron, rule. This is the optimum time for writing, public speaking, intellectual pursuits, memory, and all other forms of communication. Colors for this day are light blue, gray, green, orange and yellow. The crystals are sodalite, moss agate, opal, and aventurine. The herbs and incense are cinnamon, periwinkle, dill, sweet pea, cinquefoil and ferns.

Thursday is the day for business, politics, legalities, bargaining, good fortune, and material and fiscal wealth. The colors are blue, purple and turquoise. As you might suspect, the crystals are turquoise, sapphire, amethyst and lapis lazuli, so favored by the Egyptians. The herbs and incense for the day are saffron, cedar, nutmeg, pine, oak and cinnamon.

Friday is ruled by Freya, the Nordic Venus, goddess of love. Friday is all about beauty, love, sex, fertility, friendships and partnerships, the arts, harmony and music, and bringing the new into your life. Pale green and deep green, robin's-egg blue, pink and violet are the colors, and the crystals are emerald, pink tourmaline, rose quartz, as well as jade, malachite and peridot. The herbs and incense for Fridays are apple, lily, birch, pink rose, verbena, ivy, rose and sage.

Saturday is a time for protection, discipline, duty, binding, family, manifestation and completion. Saturday's crystals are amethyst, smoky quartz, jet, black onyx, obsidian and darkest garnet. The incense, plants, and herbs for this day are ivy, oak, rue, moss, myrrh, deadly nightshade, mandrake, hemlock and wolfsbane. (Many Saturn herbs are toxic; please exercise caution when using them.)

A Lovely Night for a Moon Dance – Saturn Day Night Fever

Here is a pagan party plan which is wonderful for weekend evenings. You can add many embellishments such as important astrological or lunar happenings, but you should gather your friends or coven and celebrate life any Saturday night of your choosing. If the weather is warm enough, have the festivities outside. Otherwise, make sure to choose an indoor space with enough room for dancing, drumming and major merriment. Ask each of your guests to bring cake, cookies and sweets of their choice along with their favorite beer, wine, mead, cider or ale and sitting cushions. Place the offerings on a center table altar and light candles of all colors. Once everyone is seated and settled, the host or designated circle leader chants:

Gods of Nature, bless these cakes.
That we may never suffer hunger.
Goddess of the harvest,
Bless this ale,
That we may never suffer thirst. Blessed be.

The eldest and the youngest should serve the food and drink to all in the circle. Lastly, they serve each other and the leader chants the blessing again. Let the feasting begin!

Sunday Spell for Welcoming Benevolent Spirits

We can all use more angels in our lives. Some angels take human form such as helpful friends or a thoughtful co-worker who are always there when you need them. Still others hover above in the ether and can be summoned with the right spell. Use this incantation when you need a guiding hand or angelic assistance. What you need: wind chimes, sage.

Goddess Invocation – Sowing Seeds of Change (Sunday New Moon is Optimal)

Nature is the ultimate creator. At a nearby gardening store or hardware store, get an assortment of seed packets to plant newness into your life. If your thumb is not the greenest, try a wildflower mix or poppies which are extremely hardy, grow quickly and spread, beautifying any area. They re-seed themselves, which is a lovely bonus.

On a new moon morning, draw a square in your yard with a "found in nature" wand, a fallen branch. Apartment dwellers can use a planter on a deck or a big pot for this ritual. Each corner of the square needs a candle and a special stone. I get my stones at new age bookstores, which often have the shiny tumbled versions for as little as one dollar. Mark the corners as follows:

Green candle and peridot or jade for creativity, prosperity and growth

Orange candle and jasper or onyx for clear thinking and highest consciousness

Blue candle and turquoise or celestine for serenity, kindness and a happy heart

White candle and quartz or limestone for purification and safety

Repeat this chant as you light each candle:

Greatest Selene, I turn to you to help me renew,
Under this new moon and in this old earth.
Blessings to you; blessings to me. Blessed be.

Put the seeds under the soil with your fingers and tamp them down gently with your wand, the branch, which you should also stick in the ground at this time. Water your new moon garden and affirmative change will begin in your life that very day.

Lavender Love Moonday Spell

To prepare for the week, you must first establish a self-care zone filled with loving energy not only toward yourself but others in your life. You only have room for the very best energy, so banish anything that can get in the way of the flow of positive energy. Try this herbal energy magic:

Steep lavender in hot water. Once the infusion has cooled to room temperature, dip your fingertips in the herbal tincture and anoint your temples and base of your throat, then sprinkle tiny droplets in your bedroom while intoning:

All is love and love is all
All is new here now, I say.
Make way, be gone, goodbye

All here is new, say I.
So mote it be!

Use the remainder of the lavender infusion to wash your front steps or stoop, the entry to your home, thereby clearing and cleansing the threshold of your home.

You will notice that every time you enter your home, it feels lighter and brighter thanks to the energetic de-cluttering.

Woden's Moon – Wednesday Wonder Invocation

Woden is also known as Odin, whom superhero fans now know from the wildly popular Thor movies, is at the top of the Nordic pantheon of the gods. He wields mighty power and is also associated with Mercury, with rulership of communication and keen intelligence. Woden even appears in olden Persian mythology, wherein he is credited with creating the moon on a Wednesday. Remember to offer thanks to the generous deity for gifting us our lovely lunar disk. Place dill and rosemary, two herbs for all-around mental strength and clarity, in your burning bowl. Light a yellow candle and use this to light the herbs. Patchouli incense adds power to this ritual; light this to power up your mental faculties and walk around your personal space to imbue this scent of smartness all around your work area. This will open your mind and abet your ability to create, whether your intention is to write a letter, a speech, prepare for a job interview or any project where you need to give your best. Once you feel focused, speak this spell:

I call upon you, great Woden
On this, your day
By my hand,
And with your blessing,
The fire of my mind
Burns bright,
Burns long,
Burns eternal.
Deep gratitude
On this day
Under this moon
Which you have given,
Blessings to all.

Green Thumb Thursday Spell

On a Thursday, as the moon waxes, light green and purple candles anointed with pure lotus or sandalwood oil. Place a small ivy or fern on your altar, along with a glass of fresh water containing a pearl or piece of jade. Burn a stick of sandalwood incense in a pot of soil placed at the altar's north quadrant and meditate on your hopes and dreams.

When the incense has burned down, place the plant in the larger container, then bow and pray:

As this living thing expands, so shall the power of this magic space grow.
Oh, Goddess, I dedicate my magic to you. Harm to none and only good
work from this holy place.
Blessed be.

Bury the jewel in the soil and use the water from the glass to water the plant. Keep your plant "familiar" with you. You will grow in health and power together. I also encourage you to continually revitalize your altar by adorning it with sacred objects—an iridescent feather, an egg-shaped pebble from the side of the road, a rosy pomegranate, or any other sacred object you find will make a perfect altar gift.

The Writing is On the Wall – Wednesday Waning Moon Magic

In the days of yore, people often made their own inks, thus imbuing them with a deeply personal energy. They simply went to the side of the road and gathered blackberries or pokeberries from the vines that grew there. Often a bird flying overhead will supply a gift of volunteer vines best cultivated by a fence where they can climb, making berry-picking easier. When it comes to matters of the heart, contracts, legacy letters and any document of real importance that you feel the need to make your mark upon, an artfully made ink can help you write unforgettable love letters and very memorable memorandums. This spell is best performed during the waning moon.

Gather the following for your ink recipe: a vial or small sealable bottle, dark red ink, 1/8th cup crushed berry juice, nine drops of burgundy wine, apple essential oil, and paper.

Mix the juice, wine and red ink in a small metal bowl. Carefully pour it into the vial and add one drop of the apple essence. Seal the bottle and shake gently.

Incant aloud:

By my hand, this spell is wrought.
With this ink, I will author my own destiny
And have the happy life and love, I sought.
So mote it be.

Now write the fate you envision for yourself in the near and far future using the enchantment ink and a feather for a pen. Let dry and seal it in an envelope and keep on your altar until the new moon phase. Then, by the light of a red candle, open the letter to yourself and read aloud. After, burn the paper using the candle and scatter the ashes in your garden. By the next new moon, you will begin to reap the positive plans you invoked.

Thursday's Prosperity Incantation

This spell is truly marvelous for getting a new or better-paying job. You will get the best results on a new moon or full moon Thursday night but any "Thor's Day" will do.

To prepare yourself, begin by pouring a few drops of green apple or verbena essential oil into a hot vessel of water. Breathe in the steam deeply ten times, inhaling and exhaling deeply for cleansing. Light a single green candle. As you close your eyes, meditate on your true desires. What does personal prosperity mean to you? What do you really *need*? What do you most desire?

When you are clear about your answers, focus on the candle flame while intoning:

Here and how, my intention is set.
New luck will be mine and all needs will be met.
With harm to none and plenty for all, blessed be.

After your cleansing breath meditation, perform this tried and true prosperity ritual to seal deals and bring about the new gainful employment and fiscal abundance your way.

Light a yellow-gold candle and light cinnamon incense with the candle. Place a piece of amethyst crystal by the candle and incense and repeat this incantation eight times while envisioning yourself with perfect abundance at the perfect job:

I see the perfect place for me; I see a place of plenty.
Upon my heart's desire, I am set.
Prosperity comes to me now.

Place the vessel of water on your alter and let it cool. At midnight, pour the prosperity potion on the roots of a nearby tree.

The Charmed Life: Thriving Thursdays

We all need to give ourselves a health and happiness boost. This spell aimed at abetting menial and emotional well-being is best performed when the hardy spirit of Thor is in ascendance. On any Thursday, take a blue candle, dress it with cedar or bergamot oil, and say nine times:

Fears and woes — I take respite;
Worries and cares — you're out of sight.
Stronger and happier, I will grow each day;
My soul has found its way.

If you do this for several weeks, your friends will notice as your health blooms and you simply beam with a bright, jolly and renewed sense of self and well-being.

The Supernatural Spectrum – Candle Color Magic

For a peaceful home, burn blue candles on Thursday.

To overcome fear, burn red candles on Sunday.

For inner peace, burn silver candles on Monday.

For self confidence, burn red candles on Sunday.

For kindness and compassion, burn pink candles on Friday.

For physical well-being, burn green candles on Friday.

To overcome regret or guilt, burn white candles on Saturday.

For mental clarity, burn yellow candles on Wednesday.

To let go of anger, burn orange candles on Tuesday.

For success at work, burn green candles on Friday.

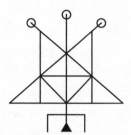

Chapter 6:

The Moon is a Silver Coin: Money Magic Secrets and Incantations for True Abundance

A s a tarot reader and spiritual advisor, the two most common requests are for help with love and money. Usually, people need advice and guidance on both. I, also, seek knowledge and wisdom on these two all-important topics and have found that my medieval studies before and after college have been the most informative. No matter how modern your money problems may be, it is the wisdom of the past that will help you the most. The wise women and hedge witches of olden times are rooted in such real magic, when ensuring abundance wasn't about your desire for a new car or a nice vacation but actual survival—keeping food on the table and a store of goods to get you through the long winter. These elders used the night sky as their guide and applied lunar insight on a daily basis. These wise women harnessed the power of the moon to take care of their village and loved ones. You can do the same.

Moons of Manifestation

You can fill your coffers and reduce your stress by mind. When the moon is waxing, growing from a new moon state towards full, this is a time to sow seeds and plant crops, and cast spells for attracting things into your life. Use this lunar waxing time to attract the new into your life. When the moon is waning, gradually getting smaller from a full moon state back into a new moon, this is a time to harvest crops, cut your hair, and shed that which you no longer want in your life.

Prosperity Altar: Using the Laws of Attraction

The full moon is the time for fomenting your intentions and seeing them to fruition. You can increase your prosperity by remembering one of the most basic principles of prosperity: by giving, so shall you receive. To create a prosperity altar, consecrate the area with sea salt. Cover a low table with green and gold altar cloths or scarves and place matching candles on it. Each day, "recharge" your altar with an altar gift such as flowers, jade or other green crystals, golden flowers, scented amber resin, and coin-shaped pebbles.

Mint Money Bags
(Moon in Taurus, Cancer or Capricorn)

Rather than chasing money or possessions, you can simply draw them toward you with wisdom from days gone by. A tiny green pouch filled with the herbs chamomile and mint, three cinnamon sticks, one silver dollar and a green stone—peridot or a smooth mossy-colored pebble of jade—would be perfect. The untrained eye might perceive this as a bag of weeds and rocks but any kitchen witch knows this is a powerful tool for creating powerful change into your life and attracting good fortune.

Prepare your attraction pouch during a waxing moon; the strongest power would be when the sun or moon is in Taurus, Cancer or Capricorn. Hold the pouch over frankincense incense and as the smoke blesses the bag, you speak:

The moon is a silver coin; this I know.
I carry lunar magic with me everywhere I go.
Blessings upon thee and me as my abundance grows.

Carry this power pouch with you as you go about your way—to work, to the store, on your daily walks, to social events. Soon, blessings will shower down upon you. You might even receive a gift or literally find money in your path.

Attraction Action – A Group Rite

Here is a beautifully simple way to attract money to you and your circle. Be sure to pass on some of the good fortune that has shone on you in order to keep the flow of abundance in circulation. This ritual is most effective performed at midnight on a full moon. Ask the participants to bring a green candle with their name scratched into the wax. Find the biggest green candle you can get and light it at the stroke of midnight.

Ask each ritualist to step forward and recite their name, lighting their candle from the large one. Pray aloud:

Holy Moon on this bright night!
Now is the time for fortune to shine.
Mother Moon, lend us your power
In this midnight hour.
Full moon bright, full moon's light,
Grant to us, our wish tonight.
Let abundance flow from this rite.
With harm to none, so mote it be.

Allow the candles to burn out on their own.

As they flicker under the full moon, gather the circle in a comfortable spot and talk about what you want to manifest in your lives. The more specifics in the discussion, the better. This rite bears repeating every once in a while to renew the power.

In a Pinch Prosperity Spell

Cinnamon, which you probably have a plentitude of in your kitchen cabinet, is a major source of prosperity and can even bring it about in a hurry. Thursdays are named for Jupiter, or Jove, originally Thor of Norse mythology, who represents joviality, expansion, and all things abundant. Here is a Jupiterian Thursday spell that will bring excellent opportunities your way.

Gather both cinnamon sticks and the powdered kind and place on your altar. On a Thursday, light incense, preferably cinnamon, and walk through your house, wafting the delightfully sweet smoke in every room. Light two altar candles, one brown and one green. Gather flowers, preferably yellow ones, such as daisies and adorn your altar with them. Stand in front of your natural altar and consider the wonderful, full life you are going to enjoy. Pour the cinnamon spice and sticks into a bowl and pray aloud:

This humble spice I offer to the gods who provide all.
I am grateful for all I receive, no matter how small.
Now, I find I am in need,
Blessings shall come now with great speed.
As above, so below,
The wisdom of the world shall freely flow.
To perfect possibility, I surrender.
And so it is. Blessed be to all.

Lady of the Silver Moon Charm

Put a silver coin at full moon in a bowl of water.

Look up at the moon and soak in the light.

Whisper the following spell three times:

Lovely lady of the moon, bring to me health and wealth.
Fill my pockets with silver and gold,
As much as my purse can hold.
Blessings to all; blessings to me.
Blessed be.

Green Magic – Basil Abundance Ritual

Take a few sprigs of basil before you cook and put them in a green bowl on your kitchen altar. Boil water as for tea and pour over the herb in the bowl. Now chant this medieval-inspired charm:

With bounteous hand and healthful balm,
Blessed basil, most verdurous herb
Bring me health and heart and calm.
Abundance I shall see by every deed and verb.
And so it is.

Breathe in the steam from the basil bowl and fill your lungs with the smell of prosperity. Repeat the spell once more; leave the basil bowl on your altar for 24 hours. Not only will your thinking be greatly clarified, but you will begin to see signs of your wealth increasing in one week. With basil flourishing in your herb pots, you have a ready source bursting with positive money energy.

Keep Your Moon Goddess Close

Whether you're passinate about writing code, cooking, growing plants, painting, or writing music, you can stay in touch with your favorite goddess by using a special tool that will draw her to you with the sweet-smelling smoke of sage.

Sage is hardy and sun-loving, so keep a pot of it on the windowsill. There are very simple steps to take to create a sage wand to use when you need inspiration. First, you will want to create a tight braid of materials. This braid will consist of a long fennel stalk, a twisted bundle of sage, long sticks of incense (I prefer cinnamon), and purple (for power) and gold (for money) string or thread. Before your prayers to the goddess, simply light one end of your wand and gently wave it around your head to clear your environment. Your mind will be cleared in the process, freeing the way for abundant ideas. A little sage smoke goes a long way, so you will not want to burn the entire wand at once. Keep a cup of water or a small bowl of earth on hand to extinguish your wand when you are done. Always express gratitude to the goddess for all she does for all of us.

Bay Leaf Money Magic

Harvest several leaves from your neighborhood Bay laurel tree—or just from the space rack in your cupboard—and place them inside a clear bowl on your altar overnight. In the morning, remove the leaves and let them dry in your kitchen window. Touch the water to your fingertips and touch your purse, wallet and anywhere you keep money. If you handle money at your workplace, bottle some of the bay leaf water in a tiny jar and do the same. Once the soaked leaves have dried, place in your wallet, purse and pockets, and it will attract money to you and yours. (It also repels thieves and loss of wealth.) You can also put some bay leaves in your desk at home or work to enhance prosperity for your employer, or before asking for a raise. Thursdays are the ideal day for this but try this anytime the need arises!

Prosperity herbs and plants: bay leaf, bayberry, basil, chamomile, cloves, cinnamon, honeysuckle, Irish moss, mint, strawberry leaves, Tonka beans

Lucky Charm

Another lucky charm for solvency is to take seven tiny turquoise stones and put them on your windowsill during a full moon for seven hours. Then pick up the stones, and while holding them in the palm of your hand, speak this wish-spell:

Luck be quick, luck be kind.
And by lucky seven, good luck will be mine.

Carry these lucky stones with you in a bright blue bag and be on the lookout for blessings to shower down upon you. You might receive a gift, win free services, or literally find money in your path.

Invocation for New Employment

Here is a great way get a new job. Light a gold candle and place it in a special place beside a crystal chunk of shiny gold pyrite. Repeat this incantation eight times while holding the gold in your right hand and holding a vision of yourself at the desired job:

To see what the future holds,
I must be bold.
I see the perfect job for me;
I see a place of plenty.
Upon my heart's desire I am set;
My new boss will never regret.
This job will come to me now;
Harm to none, I vow.
With harm to none, so mote it be.

Pool of Plenty: Intention Setting Spell (Full Moon is Optimal)

After any magical work involving employment, you should immerse yourself in the waters of prosperity with a money bath. This particular ritual is most effective if practiced on Thursday night during a new or full moon. Pour pine, mint or green apple essential oil into running bathwater and bathe by the light of a single green candle. Immerse yourself completely and, as you rise, close your eyes and meditate on your truest desires. What does personal prosperity mean to you? What do you really need and what do you really want? Focus on the candle flame while whispering:

The lean times are past and possibilities are vast.
Here and now, my intention is set.
New luck will be mine and all needs will be met.
With harm to none and plenty for all, so mote it be.
With thanks to the goddess who provides all.

Gratitude Spell

In your pantry and backyard, you have much that you need to attract whatever you want more of into your life—love, money, a new home, a new job, increased creativity. The jar of cinnamon on your shelf is filled with sheer potential, and not just for baking cookies or dessert. Cinnamon is a spice of abundance.

To engender greater and long-lasting positive change, perform this spell:

Take seven green votive candles, seven cinnamon sticks, and seven flat green leaves from a plant in your garden; ivy or nasturtium are excellent choices. On your kitchen table, arrange the candles in a circle, placing them on the leaves. Anoint each candle with a dab of cinnamon oil, which works swiftly, as it is ruled by Mercury—the god of speed, swift change, and fast communication whom operates in the element of air. Place the sticks in the center. At 7 a.m. or 7 p.m. for seven days, light a candle. Then incant aloud:

Luck be quick, luck be kind.
And by lucky seven, good fortune will be mine.
As above, so below,
The wisdom of the gods shall freely flow.
To perfect possibility, in gratitude I go.

Each day, at the strike of 7 o'clock, perform your ritual.

Later, you can count your blessings; there will be at least seven.

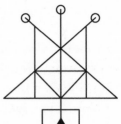

Chapter 7:

Mother Moon's Cure: The Homely Healing Arts

Centuries ago, witches were the wise women of the village, the healers and midwives who could halt a fever with a poultice or hasten the setting of bones by concocting medicinal tea. The lore of growing and gathering healing herbs has been passed down for hundreds of years. A learned witch knows which phases of the moon are best for planting seeds, how to plan your garden by the stars, and how to create spells for health and harmony. Healing spells are "earth magic." The rituals that create both soundness of body and clarity of mind are eminently practical. They are a wonderful mix of gardening, herb lore, minding the moon and sky, and heeding ancient folk wisdom. In crafting healing, you are using your magic in conjunction with the properties of the herbs, a powerful combination. It is a subtle process, growing more effective through repeated practice.

Handmade Healing Amulets: Growing Good Health

You will experience years of enjoyment from tending your garden, as Voltaire taught us in his masterpiece, *Candide*. You can share that pleasure with your friends and those you love with gifts from your garden. Your good intentions will be returned many times over. I keep a stock of small muslin drawstring bags for creating amulets. If you are a crafty witch, you can make the bags, sewing by hand, and stuff the dried herbs inside.

For courage and heart: mullein or borage

For good cheer: nettle or yarrow

For fellow witches: ivy, broomstraw, maidenhair fern

For safe travels: comfrey

For fertility: cyclamen or mistletoe

For protection from deceit: snapdragon

For good health: rue

For success: woodruff

For strength: mugwort

For youthful looks: an acorn

Amulets should be kept on your person at all times: in a pocket, in your purse or book bag, or on a string around your neck.

Hedgewitch Tinctures

Teas brewed from a single herb are commonly called "simples." I love that phrase of olden times. Experience has taught me that these simples often have the most intensity, since the very singleness of the herb gives it potency. A simple made from one of the following herbs enhances mental clarity, even clairvoyance. This will jumpstart you on your path toward any creative pursuit. Here is a recipe for a very inspired tea:

Boil one pint of spring water. Place into your favorite crockery teapot a half-ounce of any ONE of the following herbs: rosemary, mugwort, yarrow or thyme.

Steep for ten minutes and strain with a nonmetallic strainer, like cheesecloth or an inexpensive bamboo strainer. Sweeten with a little honey; I recommend clover honey because you get the added benefits of clover's lucky powers. Sip this brew while relaxing, and be inspired!

Moon Stone: Personal Power Crystal Blessing

You can perform a blessing on a single stone and keep it with you at all times. I keep an amethyst crystal chunk on my nightstand and another one that is a candleholder in my office. As a Pisces, I want my birthstone energy with me for strength, stability, and a love connection with the universe.

Choose a crystal to become your touchstone. Begin charging your crystal on your altar during a full moon. Light a white candle for purification and then place your hands on the stone. Chant thrice:

Goddess of Night, moon of this night,
Fill my stone with your white light.
Instill this stone with your magic and might;

Surround it with your loving sight.
So mote it be.

Perform this spell three nights in a row. Then you can begin to draw energy from your personal moon stone. Your sanctified stone will be a source of strength, wisdom, and love you can turn to whenever you are down and in need of a boost. And, best of all, you can take it with you.

Rejuvenation Invocation: The Water of Life

I advise any witchy gardener to have a rain barrel to make the most of stormy weather; you can water your pots of herbs and garden during sunnier days and dry spells. On the first day of the rainfall, place a blue glass bowl outside as a water-catcher. Bring it inside and place on your altar beside a lit candle. Speak:

Water of life, gift from the sky,
We bathe in newfound energy, making spirits fly!

Dip your fingers in the water and touch your forehead. Meditate upon the healing work you and your garden can do, thanks to the nurturing rainfall. Pour the water into the ground of your garden, speaking the spell one last time.

Misty Moon Potion
(Waxing Moon is Optimal)

If you are dreaming of true abundance, with the understanding that health is more important than wealth, you want to feel your best. You can bring this about with this potent potion:

- 3 drops vanilla oil

- 3 drops lavender

- 3 drops orange blossom essence

- 4 ounces pure distilled water

Pour all these into a colored glass spray bottle and shake well three times. Fifteen minutes before you retire, spray lightly on your linens, towel, and pillow case. Keep a dream journal on your nightstand so you can record details of the dreams of abundant health that will soon manifest.

Pagan Zen Pick-Me-Up
(Any Moon Phase is Optimal)

The ancient pagan art of aromatherapy owes its newfound popularity to its remarkable capacity to heal the mind and alter the emotions. To enhance your spiritual health, combine the following essential oils in a dark colored bottle with a sealable cap:

Six drops lavender oil, four drops frankincense, six drops vanilla oil, and two ounces almond oil

Light your way to a healthier outlook by burning this Pagan Zen combination in an oil lamp or, for a quick pick-me-up, dab them onto light bulbs in your home or office. A soothing, meditative smell will soon develop you.

Sandalwood Spell for Grounding (Waning Moon and New Moon)

Sandalwood, from the Sanskrit word chandana, has been used for thousands of years in India. The woody, sweet smell clears your mind and reconnects you to the earth. This simple spell can actually be used every day as prayer, or to prepare for meditation. Light a stick of sandalwood incense and "smudge" the area with the soothing smoke.

Anoint a brown candle with sandalwood oil. In scentless base oil, such as canola, olive or sesame, add:

- Six drops sandalwood oil

- Two drops lemon oil

- Two drops amber oil

Warm this concoction in a clay oil lamp or carefully heat it on the stove. When it is warm to the touch, dip your left ring finger into the oil and anoint your "third eye," located in the center of your forehead, just above the eyes.

Sitting in the cross-legged lotus position, whisper three times:

Come to me clarity, come to me peace,
Come to me wisdom. Come to me bliss.
I sit in stillness, I sit in peace.
As above, so below; and so it is.

Meditate for twenty minutes, and then massage the warmed oil into your feet. You will be utterly and blissfully grounded now.

Citrine Serenity Ceremony
(All Moon Phases)

Light a yellow candle for mental clarity, and anoint with calming and uplifting bergamot oil. Place a yellow rose in a vase to the left of the candle. To the right, place a bowl containing at least two citrine or quartz crystals.

Saffron water is made by boiling a single teaspoon of saffron from your cupboard in two quarts of distilled water. Let cool to room temperature and pour into the bowl of crystals. Put your hands together as in prayer, and dip your hands in the bowl. Touch your "third eye" in the center of your forehead, anointing yourself with the saffron water. Now, speak aloud:

Goddess great, fill me with your presence.
This night, I am whole and at peace.
Breathing in, breathing out, I feel your safe embrace.
And so it is.

Self-Blessing Spell
(All Moon Phases)

The time you take to restore yourself is precious. Morning is the optimal time to perform a self-blessing, which will help you maintain both your physical health and provide an emotional boost each and every day. Take a bundle of dried lavender grown in your kitchen garden or from a purveyor of organic herbs and place it into a muslin sack. Knead the lavender three times and breathe in the calming scent. Beginning at the top of your head, your crown chakra, pass the pouch all the way down to your feet, gently touching your other sacred chakras: throat, solar plexus, stomach and pelvis. Holding the lavender bag over your heart, speak aloud:

Gone are sorrows, illness and woe;
Here wisdom and health flows.
My heart is whole, joy fills my soul.
Blessed be me.

Hope and Healing Candle Consecration

Recently, I have been wishing and hoping for peace in this world of ours, as have most of us. I have been making, burning, and giving away candles with the word "peace" written with crystals embedded in the soft candle wax.

If possible, perform this spell during a full moon night for the greatest effect. Place your stained-glass peace candle on your altar and light rose incense, which represents love and unity. Light the candle and chant:

I light this candle for hope,
I light this candle for love,
I light this candle for unity,
I light this candle for the good of all the world
That we should live in peace. And so it shall be.

Sit in front of your altar and meditate, eyes closed, for a few minutes while visualizing peace in the world. Let the candle burn completely for full charging. Whenever the world around you feels chaotic, light this candle and meditate on a sense of peace enveloping you. And it will.

Botanical Bliss: Garden Your Way to Happiness (Waxing Moon is Optimal)

For healing, plant sage word sorrel, carnation, onion, garlic, peppermint and rosemary.

For dispelling negative energy, plant heather, hawthorn, holly, hyacinth, hyssop, ivy, juniper, periwinkle and nasturtiums.

Farming and working with plants is guided by the moon, and should take place during the waxing moon in the signs of Cancer, Scorpio, Pisces, Capricorn and Taurus.

Pendulum of Truth Invocation (New Moon is Optimal)

Many witches carry a pendulum with them at all times to help make the right decisions. I sometimes see pendulums twirling over herbs and produce at the farmers market or hovering over restaurant menus. They have recently become available at most metaphysical stores, but a lovingly handmade pendulum is imbued with more personal energy. An easy DIY way to make your own pendulum is to take a strong string or length of leather and tie a ring, gemstone, or crystal to the end. By the light of the new moon, take a bundle of sage, light one end and pass the smoke over your pendulum, "smudging" and purifying your space.

Wear the pendulum around your neck for seven days. Each night, light black candles on your altar to absorb negative energy and, holding the pendulum still, chant:

Guide me to the path of truth, O goddess hear my song.
This pendulum I charge with my energy, to judge right from wrong.
So mote it be.

On the seventh day, you can begin using your new tool. Any time you need advice before making a decision, dangle the pendulum and observe its movement—swaying from front to back means yes, left to right means no.

Love Your Mother: Spells to Heal Nature

Unlike our forebears, modern witches have to help heal Mother Earth. We are charged with crafting spells to restore and nurture the planet, which in turn nurtures us. In spring, on the Vernal Equinox, March 21, sprinkle clover leaves, ground mistletoe, and cinnamon on the ground while walking widdershins, or counterclockwise. Face north with right arm raised, and say aloud:

I call upon the great powers in the north
Bless and protect this land,
Bless and protect our beloved Mother Earth!
Harm to None. So mote it be.

Planetary Protection Charms:

Planting three red flowers in the new moon will keep trespassers off property and allow the land to return to a wild well-being. I suggest penstemon, wild roses, geraniums or nasturtiums.

To heal and guard an ailing or endangered tree, an old Celtic custom involves tying a red ribbon around the trunk and chanting:

Red for the sap-blood inside this spirit-tree,
Every Full Moon,
I will retie a cord of magic around thee.
So mote it be!

Create Your Temple Sanctuary:
Magical Mandalas and Sacred Space

Spiritual health is just as important as the other kind. Regular maintenance and what I call "inner work" is greatly abetted if you have sacred space where you feel at your best. If you don't have access to a temple space, you can create a sacred temple space in your own home. The imprint of your own creativity is vital to your personal shrine; it should be decorated with things also made by your own hand. Ideally, your windows allow sacred light to fall upon your designs. This is an artistic endeavor; you are making sacred art. If you do your best work at night, be sure to have adequate lighting. It is also a good idea to reduce the possibilities of distractions and interruptions. It is strongly suggested to turn off phones and television, to create as peaceful an environment as possible.

Bless the space in a fashion of your own choosing with your favorite incense, candles and objects that represent deepest spirituality to you. A magical mandala will greatly enhance your sacred space. The word "mandala" is from the classical Indian language of Sanskrit. Loosely translated to mean "circle," a mandala is far more than a simple shape. It represents wholeness, and can be seen as a model for the organizational structure of life itself—a cosmic diagram that reminds us of our relation to the infinite, the world that extends both beyond and within our bodies and minds.

Clarify Your Intention

Why do you want to create a mandala? Your reason is your intention, and is the focus of your ritual. One basic guideline is that the creation of a sand mandala should be "for the greater good." Some examples of reasons to create a specific mandala include:

To help create world peace

To bring renewed health to body and spirit

To bless a new home

To bless and bring joy to all people in your life

Sun: Its rays are a representation of light, energy, and life. A sun mandala will represent the positive and celebrate your life, the spark and flame of existence.

Moon: In all its phases, the moon represents the feminine and female power. Moon mandalas are wonderful for women to create in celebration of their own femininity and of woman-power throughout time. Any goddess mandala can include the symbol of the moon.

Heart: A universal symbol of love, this sweet design would make an excellent blessing to a romantic relationship or a gift to loved ones.

Triangle: It represents the Christian Holy Trinity and Egyptian spirituality and wisdom.

Downward-Pointing Triangle: It represents the "yoni yantra" and signifies the female, the element of water, and the mother and the ability to create. A mandala blessing for an expectant mother should include the downward-pointing triangle. Water signs Cancer, Scorpio and Pisces would do well to honor themselves with this design.

Double Triangle or Hexagram: In tantra, this represents all of creation, the conjunction of male and female energies. The concept of infinity is also represented by this symbol. A relationship mandala, especially in the sensual realm, will work well with double triangles. If you want to connect to the great universe, the symbol of infinity is essential. This symbol is ideal for creativity mandalas. In India, the double triangle indicates Kali in union with

Shiva, and it is also the symbol for the heart chakra. If you want to create a mandala for blessing a relationship or to open your heart, the hexagram is an excellent choice. Combining the heart symbol and hexagram would be a powerful love mandala.

Pentagram: Other names for the pentagram include the Wizard's Star, the Druid's Foot, the Witch's Cross, and the Star of Bethlehem. Wiccans have claimed the pentagram as their insignia. If you want to do a mandala for healing the earth, the pentagram will accomplish this quite nicely.

Square or Quadrangle: It is the sign of the four directions, and also the four elements and the four seasons. The square of the day also indicates the four significant times of day: sunrise, noonday, sunset, midnight. For the ancient Hindus, the square stood for order in the universe. You can use a square to invoke the four directions in this way, to honor the elements of air, earth, fire and water, and also to mark sacred time for prayer and meditation.

Octagon or Double Square: With its eight points, this is another symbol for divine order and unification. It is a good symbol for peace on earth. Essentially an eight-pointed star, the octagon is a symbol for rebirth and renewal and the wheel of the year. The octagon is believed to have magical powers, as does the pentacle or pentagram, when drawn in one line. In this case, they are believed to indicate sacred space. An octagon is a very good symbol to include in a mandala when you are embarking on a new phase of your life—a new home, job, relationship, a "new you"—that can be blessed in this manner.

Knotwork and the "Knot of Eternity": These are lovely symbols of unity. In Buddhist tradition, knotwork represents contemplation and meditation. Celtic knotwork symbolizes the eternal flow of energy and life.

Lotus: This flower represents beauty, creation, renewal, and in Buddhism, the search for enlightenment. If the lotus has twelve petals, it represents the energy of the sun. If it has sixteen petals, it is the symbol for the moon. The most spiritual mandalas will likely contain the image of the lotus.

Hold your hand over the mandala design you have drawn and visualize the light of the universe, of the sun pouring through you and through your hands to the sand and the design. If you feel a personal connection to any benevolent spirits such as angels, the Buddha, or gods or goddesses, you should call upon them to also bless your efforts and the material with their sacred energy.

You may notice a warming of your hands as you continue concentrating "in the light." Invoke aloud or pray silently to your benevolent guardians to bless your endeavor. When you are ready, take some time to look at your mandala and contemplate the image you have created. Look deeply and quietly and "receive" any insights or messages during meditation. Close the ritual by dedicating the blessing energy of the mandala to the greater good of the universe.

Color Symbology for the Chakras and Mandala Design

First, root (base of spine)   red   security, survival

Second, sacral   orange   pleasure

Third, solar plexus   yellow   divine, personal power

Fourth, heart	green	abundance, love, serenity
Fifth, throat	blue	creativity, originality
Sixth, third eye	indigo	intuitiveness, perception
Seventh, crown	violet	holy bliss, all is one

Color Connection

Color is a form of energy that can be broken down by individual vibrations. We use colors in our homes and at work to affect moods. The right colors can calm, energize, or even romanticize a setting. Colors promote many desired states of being. Anyone using color is tuning in to the vibration frequency of that particular color. Some psychics have the skills and training to read your aura; they can literally see the energy radiating out from your body.

Other colors not in the spectrum or chakra exist in crystals and stones, and are significant in their own right: brown, gray, black, white, silver and gold.

Brown: the color of humility and poverty; represents safety and the home.

Gray: the color of grief and mourning; symbolized resurrection in medieval times; gray is the first color the human eye can perceive in infancy.

Black: protection and strength; fortifies your personal energies and gives them more inner authority; symbolizes fertile, life-giving, rich earth, and nourishing rain in Africa.

White: purity, peace, patience, and protection; some cultures associate white with death.

Silver: relates to communication and greater access to the universe; indicates a lunar connection or female energy.

Gold: direct connection to God; facilitates wealth and ease.

The color spectrum is correlated with seven basic vibrations. These are the same vibrations that comprise the musical scale, and the same vibrations that are the foundation of our seven vibration chakra system. The "lightest" vibrations are at the top and the "heaviest" vibrations are at the bottom. By now you should know that the color system is composed of seven colors, all visible in the rainbow: red, orange, yellow, green, blue, indigo and violet. A great way to remember the colors is by their collective acronym, which sounds like a name: Roy G. Biv. Consult the following color guide when you are choosing a color for any aspect of your life.

Color management can help you on the most basic level each day. To combat feeling depressed, wear yellow to raise your energy level. If you have a business meeting and you want to put your colleagues at ease, wear earthy colors like brown or green. You can experiment with different combinations, too. Remember, the purpose here is to find your soul colors.

Teutonic Tonic

You will notice that many a witch appears ageless. There is a good reason for this; we manifest a lot of joy in our life, including creating potions to take excellent care of our skin for goddess-like youthfulness. This refresher is inspired by the eternally strong and beautiful deity Freya.

Combine these oils in a sealable dark blue bottle:

- 2 ounces sweet almond as base oil

- 2 drops chamomile

- 2 drops rosemary

- 2 drops lavender oil

Shake very thoroughly and prepare to anoint your skin with this invocation:

Goddess of Love, Goddess of Light, hear this prayer,
Your youth, beauty and radiance, please share. So mote it be.

Clean your skin with warm water, then gently daub with the potion. You can also make a salve or balm using my recipe if you want to turn the clock backwards. Prepare to be asked for your beauty secrets.

Flower Remedy Ritual (All Moon Phases)

Flower essences restore emotional balance and aid physical harmony. Naturopathic doctors and healers recommend using Dr. Bach's flower remedies, which were originally created from the morning dew found on flower petals. These subtle medicines are available in most health food and metaphysical stores. To know which essences are right for you, take a pendulum and write the essence names on paper in a wheel formation. Holding the pendulum in the middle, wait for it to select one name while chanting:

Spirit of the flower, help me this day
To keep disease and depression far at bay. Blessed be.

To prepare the following remedies, mix two drops of flower essence in 30 milliliters of distilled water. Take four drops of the remedy daily until your health is restored. You can also apply the remedy to your pulse points: wrists, temples, behind the ears, back of knees. You can also add it to your bath, or spray it into the air. Following is a guide to healing flower remedies:

Addiction: skullcap, oregano

Anger: nettle, blue flag, chamomile

Anxiety: garlic, rosemary, aspen, periwinkle, lemon balm, white chestnut, gentian

Bereavement: honeysuckle

Depression: borage, sunflower, larch, chamomile, geranium, yerba santa, black cohosh, lavender, mustard

Exhaustion: aloe, yarrow, olive, sweet chestnut

Fear: poppy, mallow, ginger, peony, water lily, basil, datura

Heartbreak: heartsease, hawthorn, borage

Lethargy: aloe, thyme, peppermint

Stress: dill, Echinacea, thyme, mistletoe, lemon balm

Spiritual blocks: oak, ginseng, lady's slipper

Salt of the Earth Rejuvenation Ritual (New Moon or Waning Moon)

Salts have been used to purify the body, by way of ritual rubs, since ancient times in the Mediterranean and Mesopotamia. Beauties from the biblical era utilized this simple curative of natural salts to exfoliate the skin and enhance circulation, vital to overall body health. There are wonderful imported Dead Sea salts readily available at most bath and beauty stores, or you can make your own using Goddess Glow recipes, one of the kitchen cupboard cures that follows.

To prepare for your body glow session, light a white candle, step out of your clothes and into your tub or shower, and hold the salts in the palms of both hands, praying:

Aphrodite, in your wisdom, help me reflect your image;
My body is a temple to thee, goddess.
Here, I worship today with my head and hands, heart and soul.
Blessings to all, blessings to thee, blessed be me.

Use the salts with a new loofah sponge and scrub yourself vigorously during the waning moon or new moon at midnight.

Goddess Glow
(Waxing Moon Phase)

Many witches prefer whipping up their own healing beauty magic. Here's a simple recipe for a homemade salt rub. The beauty of this recipe is that you can change the essential oils to suit your mood. For example, if you are feeling romantic or preparing for a big date night, use rose and amber oils.

Combine the following:

- Three cups Epsom salts

- One tablespoon glycerin

- Four drops lemon essential oil

- Two drop jasmine oil

- Two drop vanilla

- One drop neroli oil (made from orange blossoms)

Mix well and store in a colored glass jar with a tight lid. Use these salts with the Salt of the Earth body purification ritual to help exfoliate your skin and give you a goddess glow.

Hedge Witch Herbal Healer
(Dark Moon Phase)

In the days of old, the village doctors were elder women, and quite a few utilized the knowledge of hedge witches who knew all the plants of field and forest. For an immune system boost, crush a mixture of equal parts (½ cup each) rosemary, lemon peel, lavender, and the petals of red roses. Place the crushed herbs in a sealable colored glass jar filled with almond or sesame oil, ideally twelve ounces. After seven days on a windowsill, exposed to both the sun and the dark moon, strain and place the infused oil into the jar. Speak this chant aloud:

In this dark moonlight, I will see
That I release anything that ails me.
With the wisdom of the crones of old,
All the blessings of this world unfold.

You now have a hearty supply of homemade healing oil to use in the bath, or to rub on your pulse points: temples, wrists, backs of knees, and behind the ears. As soon as you feel slightly rundown, one application should make a difference. Be sure and whisper thanks to the hedge witches who passed down this sacred healing knowledge.

Plant Infusions That Comfort and Heal

Many enthusiasts enjoy several cups a day of their favorite herbal infusion, which is a large portion of herb brewed for at least four hours and as long as ten. I recommend one cup of the dried herb placed in a quart canning jar and filled with freshly boiled water. After the steeping, strain with a non-metallic method, such as cheesecloth or bamboo. Herbal Infusions can be made with the leaves and fruits which provide the magical and healing aspects of this comforting concoction. Many of the favorite kitchen witch herbs contain minerals, antioxidants and phytochemicals, including the list herein. Roots, leaves, flowers, needles and seeds can all be used—depending on which fruit or herb is chosen to be the base. There are some cases when all parts of the plant can be used in some manner, and at others only one or two parts are safe—it is important, when creating a blend from scratch, that the creator has researched ingredients to understand what parts can be used.

What do you need to attend in your life now? This list of herbs and associations can be your guide; one of the smartest ways to approach this methodology is to brew right before bedtime, and you will awaken to a freshly infused herb. Some of the most popular herbs and fruits used to create infusions are:

Anise Seeds & Leaves – soothes cramps and aches

Caraway Seeds – aids in romantic issues, helps with colic

Catnip Leaves – makes women even more attractive

Chamomile Flowers – helps with sleep, good for abundance

Dandelion Leaves – makes wishes come true

Echinacea – makes the body strong

Ginseng Root – increases men's vigor

Nettle Leaves – lung function, hex breaking

Peppermint Leaves – rids tummy discomfort, cleansing

Pine Needles – increases skin health as well as financial health

Rose Hip Fruit – packed with vitamin C and can halt colds and flu

Sage Leaves – purifies energy, antibiotic

Skullcap Leaves – prevents insomnia, cures St. John's Wort, anti-depressant protection

Thyme Leaves – antiseptic, a protectant

Yarrow Flowers – reduce fever, bring courage and good luck

Crystal Cures for Every Day of the Week

Gemstones and crystals have healing powers based on ancient belief systems passed down from the Chaldeans and metaphysicians of the old world. Among the treasure trove of knowledge they passed down are these crystal cures:

Sapphire has violet energy; worn first on Saturday on the middle finger of the right hand two hours before sunset, the stone is said to be curative for kidneys, epilepsy, tumors and sciatica.

Diamonds, containing rays of indigo light, are for eyes, nose, asthma, laziness and drunkenness, especially if worn on the right pinkie on Friday with the waxing moon. Worn on Sundays, diamonds enhance spiritual understanding when worn on the left ring finger.

Emerald has green light rays and can help with the heart, ulcers, cancer, asthma, and influenza, when worn on the right side pinkie on Wednesday two hours after dawn. On Tuesdays, wear it on the other hand for calm, sound sleep and to repel bad dreams and nightmares.

Pearls radiate orange rays and operate as a curative for work on Monday mornings. They help with insanity, diabetes, colic and fever.

Topaz has blue rays and helps with laryngitis, paralysis, hysteria, scarlet fever and assorted glandular disorders if worn on the right ring finger on Thursday mornings.

Pomona's Skin-Preserving Potion (Full Moon Phase Optimal)

Pomona is beloved as the apple goddess and protectress of orchards. Associated with abundance, the flowering of nature, youth and beauty, her splendor is still celebrated every year in European festivals. One way to retain our blossoming beauty is to take good care of our skin and heighten the health of our complexions with this goddess-blessed prescription for eternal youth. Add the following essential pure oils into six ounces of scentless base oil, such as sesame:

- Two drops apple

- Two drops sweet almond

- Two drops rosemary

- Two drops chamomile

- Two drops eucalyptus

- Two drops rosemary

- Two drops lavender

Combine thoroughly and place the mixture into a dark glass jar with a secure lid; shake it before application. Before you anoint your skin each night, utter this spell:

Pomona, blessed goddess of the groves,
We thank you for the fruits of the trees
And the flowers of the fields.
Bringer of honey, bounty and beauty.
We thank you for the flower of youth
From this day forward. So mote it be.

Balm for the Spirit: DIY Healing Salve (Waxing Crescent Moon is Optimal)

Any body or herbal oil can be turned into a salve with the addition of wax. When the moon is waxing is especially a perfect time for spiritual growth. The ratio for a body salve is three ounces coconut oil to one ounce of beeswax. If you have a pot of the herb rosemary, pick some fresh leafy stems and crush. Take a fresh lemon, peel it and grind the peel in your mortar and pestle until broken up into fine little pieces. Mix the rosemary and lemon peel together and give one last grind. Use a double boiler to heat the oil slowly and wax until completely melted. Test the viscosity of your salve by pouring a dab onto a cold plate. If satisfied with the consistency, pour off into jars to cool. If you need to add more wax, now is the time to do it.

Balms are simply salves with the addition of essential oils. Add two drops of eucalyptus essential oil and two drops of lemon oil when mix is still warm. Sprinkle in the finely crushed rosemary and lemon peel into the mix, stir well and seal to preserve the aroma. This balm will have a wonderfully calming effect anytime you use it, and can be rubbed on your temples when you need to reduce stress. It is also really good for your skin. I recommend Sunday night baths, where you slather on the balm before stepping into a hot bath. Take a washcloth and massage your skin, then lie back and relax for twenty minutes. When you drain the tub, your stress will also empty out and you can start your week afresh and ready to handle anything that comes your way.

Soak Your Soul Replenishment Rite (New Moon Phase is Optimal)

To rid yourself of negative emotions, try this purification bath. Draw a warm bath at noon when the sun is at its healing peak, and add the essential oils into the water as it flows from the faucet:

- Two drops rosemary for calm

- One drop peppermint for stimulation

- One drop lavender for energy cleansing

- Three drops thyme to relieve mental exhaustion

As you soak and steam, repeat this prayer four times.

Sadness I release you – goodbye.
Fatigue, I release you – goodbye.
I greet this day anew, I great my life renewed.
Blessed be.

Food is Magic: Color Medicine
(All Lunar Phases)

Color has a profound effect on our psychological and physical health. Consider carefully the colors that surround you; each of us have special colors that encourage sound body and mind. For example, if you have a weight issue and lack ambition or energy, you may need more orange in your life. Wear orange clothes and eat foods associated with orange, such as red plums and wax beans. Here are some basic color connections:

Violet is associated with sentiment, melancholy, and religious devotion and can be enhanced by eating chocolate, thyme, and scallops.

Orange, associated with abundance and ebullience, can be absorbed through oranges, squash, red plums, yeast and wax beans.

Yellow is connected to the renown, wealth and power, and excellence, and is best ingested through pumpkin, cheese, rye, oats, lettuce and beer.

Green, the color of everlasting life, friendship and optimism, is concentrated in beef, alfalfa, endive and grapes.

Blue relates to humility, faith and innocence, and is the mainstay of mint, garlic, radishes, sage, turnips, and peppers.

Red, associated with aggression, success, and control, is best absorbed through cabbage, bacon, cherries, lemons, tomatoes and paprika.

Kitchen Witch Alchemy

Marigold blossoms gathered at high noon will raise your energy level.

Lettuce juice (made in a juicer or food processor) rubbed on your temples and forehead will dispel sleeplessness.

Holly was once believed to repel lightening.

Hazel branches make excellent wands and divining rods. Used like pendulums, they help you answer questions.

Garlic guards against evil spirits, disease and bad weather.

Cyclamen eases the pain of grief.

Cucumber peel placed on your temple and forehead cures headaches.

Dragons' Lair Safety Spell (Waning Moon is Optimal)

After an illness or any event wherein you feel the need to rid your home of unhealthy energy, head to your metaphysical five and dime and gather these essences. Anoint your home in order to return grace to your space and protect you from harm. Simply rub any one of the following essential oils, undiluted, on your doorjamb: cinnamon, clover, cypress, dragons blood, frankincense.

Walk through the door and close it securely. Take the remaining essential oil and anoint every other door and window. At the witching hour, midnight, light anointed white candles and place them in every doorway and windowsill. Sing:

My home is my temple,
Here I will live and love and be healed.
And so it is by magic sealed.

Clary Sage Clarity Incantation
(Any Friday Night)

Here is a handy spell for physical well-being as well as a self-esteem boost. For this witchy approach to preventive medicine, take a green candle on a Friday, dress it with clary sage oil, and speak the following three times:

My health is mine, under this moon divine.
I choose to be well in this healthy body I dwell.
No more pain and strife, vital breath of life.
Harm to none; health to me.
So mote it be.

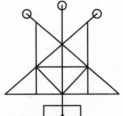

Chapter 8:

Spells to Attract, Create and Keep Love in Your Life

Like many of you, love spells were my first. At the age of fourteen, I cast my first, and soon my best friend was the object of amorous attention from a previously disinterested suitor. Since then, I have had many years and ample opportunity to perfect this most joyous aspect of the craft. I have happily watched these spells kindle and keep love's passion alive time and time again. Ask any metaphysician, and she will tell you the most common requests for help involve matters of the heart. Witchcraft is based in the knowledge that our destinies lie in our own hands, even where love is concerned. Why suffer the slings and arrows of romance gone wrong when you can do something about it? Below are lots of ideas for magical workings so you have a life you love and a life *filled* with love.

Dreamy Passion Potion

If you are dreaming of real romance, you can bring about visions of your true love to come with this potent potion:

- 3 drops rose oil

- 3 drops lavender

- 3 drops neroli, orange blossom essence

- 4 ounces pure distilled water

Pour all these into a colored glass spray bottle and shake well three times. Fifteen minutes before you retire, spray lightly on your linens, towel, and pillow case. Keep a dream journal on your nightstand so you can record details of the great love that will soon manifest.

New Moon Love Connection

If you are looking for love, perform this rite and you will soon find a lover to satisfy your needs. On the night of the next new moon, take two pieces of a pink or red crystal—rose quartz will do nicely—and place them on the floor in the center of your bedroom. If you are lucky enough to have two garnets of rough rubies or pink tourmaline, by all means use two of those heart stones.

Light one pink and one red candle and speak this love and life-affirming chant:

Beautiful crystal I hold this night,
Flame with love for my delight,
Goddess of Love, I ask of you,
Guide me in the path that is true.
Harm to none as love comes to me.
This I ask and so it shall be.

Within a fortnight, you shall receive some kind of communication from a potential love interest. It could be a handsome stranger at a coffee shop who can't take his eyes off you, or a shy bookworm at a literary reading. Be on the lookout and let your intuition be your guide.

Two Hearts Beat As One

Many crystal shops and New Age stores now feature heart-shaped rocks. The next time you see heart-shaped amethyst crystals, buy two right away and give one to your true love. The gift of an amethyst heart will ensure a happy life together and good fortune shared. Sweet!

Sacred Space for Love: Altar of Affection

To prepare for new relationships and deepen the expression of feeling and intensity to your love life, create a center from which to renew your romantic spirit. Here you can concentrate your energy, clarify your intentions and make wishes come true. If you already have an altar, incorporate some special elements, such as red candles or red crystals, or anything associated with Venus, like copper or a seashell to enhance your sex life. Your altar can sit on a low table, a big box, or any flat surface dedicated to magic. One friend of mine has her sex altar at the head or her bed. Begin by purifying the space with a sage smudge stick—a bundle of sage that you burn as your pass it through the space. Then cover your altar with a large red silk or silk-like fabric. Place two red candles at the center of your altar and place a soul mate crystal—two crystals naturally fused together—at the far right corner of the altar. These

are widely available at metaphysical stores. Anoint your candles with jasmine and neroli oil. Also keep the incense you think is sexiest on your altar. Place fresh Casablanca lilies in a vase and change them the minute they begin to fade. Lilies are heralded as exotic and erotic flowers, prized for their seductive scent.

Light of Love Altar Dedication

Light candles and incense and dab the jasmine and essential oils above your heart. Speak aloud:

I light the flame,
I fan the flame,
Each candle I burn is a wish.
My lust will never wane.
I desire and I will be desired.
Harm to none, so mote it be.

Bed Blessing

Anoint your bed with this special charm. In a red cup, mix a half-teaspoon of jasmine oil and a half-teaspoon of rose oil. Take a cotton ball and dip it into the bliss oil. Touch it to your clean sheets seven times from where you rest your head to the feet, for each chakra point. Then speak aloud:

In this bed, I show my love.
In this bed, I share my body.
In this bed, I give my heart.

In this bed, we are as one.
Here, my happiness lies as I give and live in total joy.
Blessed be to me and thee.

Now, lie down and roll around in the bed. After all, that is what it is for!

Prepare the Way for Love In Your Life

Surely one of the main reasons for clearing space in your home and bedroom is to make room for a happy love life. Before you attempt to enhance your prospects for love, you need to improve the flow of *chi*, or life energy, in the environment where you express your love. Try any of all of the following to help you improve the chi:

Remove all pictures of yourself where you are alone.

Remove all empty cups, jars, vases, and bottles.

Remove all photographs of past lovers, or at least relegate them to another room.

Make sure that decorative accessories are in even numbers, not in odds or in triplets. This pertains to candles, frames, pillows and lamps.

Display special feng shui love symbols, such as an open red fan, a pair of crystal lovebirds, and two red hearts. On your bed, you should use rich, silky, and extremely comfortable fabrics and colors. Also be extravagant when it comes to pillows—the more the merrier. But remember to have even numbers, not odd ones, which disrupt your "love chi."

Creating Space for Love in Your Home: A Relationship Corner

As you walk into your bedroom, the relationship corner will be the back right corner. Your love and sex energy have to be nurtured there, so you might as well consider placing your altar there to serve as your personal erotic wellspring.

Look at this area with a fresh eye—what is cluttering your love corner with dead energy? Half-empty perfume bottles or near-empty cosmetic bottles could be impairing your relationship energy. You must clear unhappiness out of this space and clear the area of any clutter by getting rid of all unnecessary objects and tidying up.

To cleanse the area, ring a hand bell anywhere clutter has accumulated, giving special attention to your bed and pillows. Here are a few tips:

Never bring old pillows into a new home. Old pillows can cause poor sleep and bad dreams. They can carry old sexual energy and can kill a relationship.

Never place your bed in the center of a room, as this will cause anxiety and get in the way of a healthy sex life.

Never have the foot of the bed facing the door, as this brings very bad luck.

To keep your lovemaking fresh, always make the bed and change the linens often.

Place these objects in your bedroom to attract loving energy:

- 2 rose quartz crystals of equivalent size

- Pink, orange, or red fabric

- 2 red candles

- Images of two butterflies or two lovebirds

Amorous Herbs Love Charm

Many a witchy woman has enjoyed the fruits of long-lasting love by reciting the following charm while mixing rye and pimento into a dish shared with her object of affection. While stirring in these amorous herbs, declaim:

Rye of earth, pimento of fire
Eaten surely lights desire.
Serve to he whose love I crave,
And his heart I will enslave!

Sweetheart Tea

Here is a quick recipe to create exactly the right mood for a dreamy evening:

- Stir together in a clockwise motion:

- 1 ounce dried and pulverized rosehips

- ½ ounce peppermint

- ½ ounce dried lemon balm

You can store this in a tin or colored jar for up to a year for those special evenings. When you are ready to brew the tea, pour boiling water over the herbs, two teaspoons for every cup of water. Say the following spell aloud during the five minute steeping and picture your heart's desire:

Herbal brew of love's emotion
With my wish I fortify
When two people share this potion
This love shall intensify
As in the Olde Garden of Love.

Sweeten to taste with honey and share this luscious libation with the one you love.

Glamour Gloss Enchantment: Anointed Lips

From time immemorial, witches have enchanted with their magical beauty. That is because we know how to supplement Mother Nature's gifts. Before a special evening, employ a "kiss of glamour" by adding one drop of clove oil to your favorite pot of lip gloss and gently stir in, saying aloud three times:

The ripest fruit,
The perfect petal
Each kiss is a spell of utmost bliss
And so it is.

This will make your lips tingle in a delightful way and give your kisses a touch of spice. The lucky recipient of your affection will be spellbound.

Spellbinding Kisses – A Ritual for Romance

A remarkable kiss is a gateway to ecstasy. A kiss provokes the senses, excites the heart, and offers the singular gift of yourself. Here is a list of kisses from the Indian book of love, the *Kama Sutra*:

Bent kiss – the classic movie-style smooch where the lovers lean into each other.

Throbbing kiss – touches your lover's lips with her tongue and places her hands on her lover's hands.

Turned kiss – One kisser turns up the face of the beloved by holding the head and chin before bestowing affection.

Pressed kiss – One lover from below touches the lower lip with both lips.

Greatly pressed kiss – taking the lip between two fingers, touching the lip with the tongue, then applying great pressure with lips upon lips in an emphatic kiss.

Dressed to Thrill: Charging Your Jewelry with Enchantment

Before a special date night or big evening event, you can enhance your own energy field with jewelry magic. Charging a gem or crystal imbues it with your intent. Upon charging your jewelry, you can use it in spellwork or anytime you want to surround yourself with the magic you put into the gemstones. While picturing your truest wish and hope, and what you ultimately want to achieve through this process, anoint a candle with an essential oil that most expresses your energy. Perhaps it is rose or, as in my case, amber.

Begin by lighting the candle and gazing into the flame. Then, place the piece of jewelry in front of the candle and say aloud,

Into this jewelry, I imbue my essence
Into these stones, lies the power of this blessed earth.
This gem of great hue is charged until my magic is through.
With harm to none, so mote it be!

You can further empower the jewel by scratching your desire into the wax of the candle. Then, each time you burn the candle, place the gem before it and think upon your quest.

New Moon Crystal Shrine

To enchant all of your jewelry, you need to create an altar for this express purpose. You can prepare the way for letting crystal and gem magic into your life, and focusing your desires and dreams, with a crystal-magic altar. If you already have an altar in place, incorporate some of the following elements. The more you use your altar, the more powerful your spells will be.

Your gem-magic altar can be a low table, the top of a chest, or even a shelf. First, you must purify the space with the smoke of a sage bundle. This is called smudging, and is essential in clearing energy to make way for magic. You can use wild sage or purchase it at any herb store or metaphysical five and dime.

Once you have smudged the space, cover your altar with your favorite fabric; I recommend the color white. Place a candle in each corner. I prefer candles of many colors to represent the rainbow array of gems. Place gems and crystals of your choice around the candles. Rose quartz is a heart stone, and fluorite is a calming crystal, so these are good choices for grounding yourself, particularly if your altar is in your bedroom, as many are! Add to the altar fresh flowers, incense you simply love to smell, and any objects that have special meaning to you. Some folks place lovely shells or feathers they have found in their paths or on the beach, and others use imagery that is special, like a goddess statue or a star shape. The most important point is that your altar be pleasing to your eye and your sensibilities. You should feel that it represents the deepest aspects of you as a person.

Ideally, you will bless your altar on a new moon. Light the candles and incense, and say aloud:

Here burns happiness about me,
Peace and harmony are in abundance,
Here my happiness abounds.
Gems and jewels—these bones of the earth
Bring love, prosperity, health and mirth.

Be it ever thus that joy is the light
That here burns bright.
Blessed be!

You have now consecrated your altar. It will ease your spirit anytime and become your power source. Your altar connects you to the earth of which you and all gems and crystals are a part. Your altar will connect you to the crystal magic that has now entered your life. Whenever you want to add a dash of magic or a supernatural sparkle to a stone or piece of jewelry, you can place it on your altar for seven days. On the seventh day, wear the jewelry and bewitch everyone you encounter! Remember that your level of clarity and concentration will be reflected in the jewel's power.

Now, enjoy your sacred stones.

Love Goddess Invocation

The Goddess of Love, Venus, rules this most popular day of the week, Friday. Small wonder this is the night for a tryst. To prepare yourself for a night of lovemaking, you should take a Goddess bath with the following potion in a special cup or bowl. I call mine the Venus Vial. Combine:

- *One cup sesame oil*

- *Six drops orange blossom oil*

- *Four drops gardenia oil*

Stir with your fingers six times, silently repeating three times:

I am daughter of Venus, I embody love.
My body is a temple of pleasure,
And I am all that is beautiful. Tonight,
I will drink fully from the cup of love.

Pour the Venusian mixture into a steaming bath and meditate on your evening plans. As you rise from your bath, repeat the Venus spell once more.

Don't use a towel, but allow yourself to dry naturally. Your lover will compliment the softness of your skin, and indeed, you will be at your sexiest. The rest is up to you.

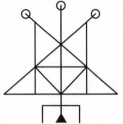

Chapter 9:

Gods and Celestial Goddesses: Lunar Lore and Spiritual Correspondences

When you undertake your own spellwork, you can pull from the wealth of the world's mythologies and create original rites based on the merging of your own intention and the deity's domain. When you call upon the gods and goddesses in your circles and ceremonies, you will need to have an understanding of their realms—know thy divinity. You should feel drawn to whomever you invoke. If you feel inclined toward a certain deity, do your homework and find out everything you can. Discretion and caution should be exercised anytime you call upon the aid of celestial beings. Kali, for example is a dark goddess associated with destruction and should never be invoked for love and harmony! Similarly, Mars is the god of war and would not be called into a peace ritual. You can use the power of the gods and goddesses in very practical ways. A dear friend who was recently laid off in a corporate restructuring researched the rites of Lakshmi, the Hindu goddess of prosperity, to invoke her generosity. A man looking for physical love could invoke the lusty Arcadian pipe-paying god, Pan. I strongly advise common sense and excellent manners in any dealings with deities and denizens of the mythical realm.

Domestic Goddesses

A form of magic handed down from antiquity is to have a domestic goddess figure in your home; archaeologists have found them amongst the most ancient artifacts. It is a wonderful energy generator to have such a figurine decorating your home altar. The most important consideration is to choose the divinity with whom you feel the deepest connection.

Which of these beneficent beings do you identify with?

Agnayi – For the Indian subcontinent, she is the equivalent of Vesta as a domestic fire goddess.

Ashnan – Here we have a Sumerian grain goddess and protector of the fields. She is depicted in Babylonian imagery from ancient times as a beautiful young woman handing worshipful men a single stalk of grain.

Athena – The wisdom goddess also rules over battle. Call upon her to help resolve any disagreements. Under her domain is the owl and also olive trees. She stopped wars in ancient times with the offerings of an olive branch.

Bast – Egypt's cat goddess who protected the lands. Bast has childbirth, healing, passion, pleasure, happiness and, of course, cats under her sphere of influence. Bast can come into your life in the form of a stray cat, a familiar, and can become a real guardian for your hearth and home.

Brigid – This Celtic solar goddess of poetry, smithcraft and healing existed long before the Catholic Church adopted her and canonized her as a saint. She is a protectress of all animals and children. Brigid can be invoked to bless your kitchen tools—pots, pans and knives can all have the strength of this bright being, forged by the fire of the sun.

Cerridwen – I was named in honor of an aspect of this Triple Goddess. She is of deep elder wisdom. In Welsh legend, Cerridwen represents the crone, which is the darker aspect of the goddess. She has powers of prophecy, and is the keeper of the cauldron of knowledge and inspiration in the Underworld. She is a mother goddess who makes sure to feed her followers and minds the fields.

The Eye Goddess – This most ancient of Mediterranean deities is depicted as an all-seeing eye and represents justice. No transgression can be hidden from the eye goddess. Dating back to 3500 B.C.E., she is often depicted as a single, unblinking eye. Anytime you need the truth brought to light, call up her. She can also protect from thieves by hanging her eye in your windows; she is an excellent resident in your magical kitchen. She is mistaken for the "evil eye," but is a benevolent presence who will watch out for you and yours 24/7.

Hathor – This "cow goddess" represents life, beloved in ancient Egypt for her ability to bring fertility. Hathor was also associated with royalty, and her priests were artists, dancers, trained midwives and seers. As the celestial cow, she held the golden disk of the sun between her horns. Hathor's other sacred animals include the lion, cobra, falcon and the hippopotamus. The sacred sistrum, a rattle used in ritual, was used to summon her. Mirrors were also her sacred tool. During spring rains and floods, you can stage a ritual dance for her to sanctify the joy of life and bless your newly planted gardens.

Juno – The Latin word for a female soul is *juno*, and Romans depended on this generous presence to watch over the daughters of the earth; she is regarded as the mother of all women and can be invoked for any magical gathering of women. Her special domain is as a protector of brides. When preparing feasts and cakes for wedding nuptials, ask Juno to bring her brightest blessings.

Persephone – Daughter of Athena, Persephone is bidden to spend half her time in the underworld with her husband, Hades. She is a harbinger of the change to the warmer seasons, as she rises from the dark world after the winter seasons, bringing spring and the growing season with her. The pomegranate is her significator. Invoke her for rites of spring.

Thalassa is a benevolent Greed goddess of the oceans, and part of a great pantheon of the seas including fresh water lake and river goddesses. She is invoked by individuals seeking to usher in change and self-transformation.

Sea Change- Releasing Ritual

A bath blessing that will both relax and purify you is a rare and wonderful thing. To prepare yourself, place one quart of rough sea salt or Epson salts in a large bowl. Add the juice from six freshly squeezed lemons, 1/2 cup of sesame oil, and a few drops of rose and jasmine oils. Stir until the mixture is completely moistened. You can add more sesame oil if necessary, but do not add more lemon, as it will make the mixture overly astringent and potentially irritating to your skin.

When your tub is one-third full, add one-quarter of the salt mixture under the faucet. Breathe in deeply ten times, inhaling and exhaling fully before you do this recitation. You may start to feel a tingling at the crown of your head. The water should still be running when you proclaim:

Thalassa, O Harmonious One,
Goddess and mistress, I ask your guidance.
Remove from me any impurities
Of heart, spirit, and mind. I open myself to you.
My wish is to once again become whole,
Free of pain, sadness, and all that is better in me.

When the tub is full, it is time to step inside and breathe deeply ten more times. Repeat the prayer to the sea goddess Thalassa, and use the rest of the salt to gently massage your body. Rest and rejuvenate as long as you like, allowing yourself to feel refreshed and renewed by the ministrations of this Greek goddess from whom eloquence, inspiration and blessings flow.

Designing Your Own Water Rituals

From the depths of your imagination, you can create a water ritual of your own by invoking other water deities. By inviting the energy of water into your sacred space, you will find the words will flow into you as you fashion ceremonial language appropriate to that god or goddess.

You can create your own ceremonies and spells to call forth the power of water for psychic development, such as dream work, emotional balance, healing, creativity, joy, love and letting go.

Water Deities

Lakshmi, also called Padma, is associated with all forms of wealth and abundance, both spiritual and material. It is said that Lakshmi can be found in gems and jewels, money, newborn babies, and in all cows. She is depicted floating on a lovely lotus blossom.

Naiads are freshwater nymphs that inhabit various bodies of water such as lakes, rivers and springs. Naiads have the power to seduce, inspire, heal and tell the future. You will do best by calling forth their gentle energy for healing rituals.

Poseidon is the Greek god of oceans and can use his might to create tidal waves, earthquakes,and typhoons. You should always appease Poseidon when you travel over water with an offering of olive oil; pour a few drops into the sea and you will enjoy smooth sailing all the way. His consort is Amphitrite, the Queen of the Sea.

Nereus, the "old man of the sea" from Greek mythology, is an oracle. You can invoke Nereus to inquire about the future, and for safety during travel by water.

Lunar Goddesses of the World:

Alkmene is the mortal mother of legendary Greek hero Hercules. Her name means "might of the moon."

Candrea is the Indonesian deity from a love story about princess Candra Kirana of Kediri. Candra was the incarnation of Dewi Ratih, goddess of love, and her name means "glowing like the moon."

Io, this Greek word for "the moon," comes from the mythological story of the priestess of Hera, who was loved by Zeus. Fittingly, the moon of Jupiter was named for her.

Luna is the Roman name for a moon goddess and means "moon."

Marama is a mythic Polynesian lunar goddess whose name has come to mean moon.

Selena is the Latinate form of the Greek name Selene, meaning "moon," and also refers to the mythic moon goddess.

Summoning the Gods: Invoking Help from the Heavens

Here is a selection of male deities to choose from in your ritual work. Included are some of the more commonly invoked gods, and also some rare and obscure powers to consider for ceremonies and incantations. There are many rich resources for further study, such as mythology, which is a real tapestry of humankind's deepest truths, eternal struggles and victories. I have learned many stories that have inspired and enriched my spiritual practices, from books such as *Bullfinch's Mythology*, Robert Graves's *The White Goddess,* and James G. Frazer's *The Golden Bough*. Reading more about the history and folklore of deities will give you ideas and inspiration for rituals of your own creation. The namesake of a Celtic goddess, I love exploring myths of old and applying the wisdom to my modern way of life. Our forebears passed a treasure trove of knowledge to us.

Adonis: God of Truth and Beauty

He is the god of love, and partner of the goddess of love, Aphrodite. Adonis is also an herbal deity with domain over certain plants and flowers, representing earth, fertility and health. He is often invoked for love rites and spells and can help the querent discover whether a potential lover is true or unfaithful. Ask Adonis for help with your gardens and for healing. He is a real helpmate.

Apollo: Brother of Artemis

He is the god of music and the arts and brother to Artemis, the Greek goddess of the moon and the hunt. If you are an artist or musician, ask Apollo to help you with the creative process or invoke him to banish writer's block.

Cernunnos: Wild Man Spirit

He is the Horned God of the Celts, sometimes called Herne the Hunter. Cerunnos is a virile figure and represents man's sexual power. He is the one to call on for animal magic, fertility and any earth or environmental ceremonies you want to create to represent the wild man's spirit.

Dagon: Oracular Fish God

He is the fishtail god of the Phoenicians, symbolizing the sea and rebirth. Originally a corn god, Dagon protects against famine and is also a god for oracles. He can be called on in water, gardening, food rituals and the celebration of life. Pisceans should familiarize themselves with this half-man, half-fish god when creating original rituals, and should ask for Dagon's aid in divination.

Ganesha: He Keeps Obstacles Out of Your Way

This elephant-headed Hindu god of good fortune is the "remover of obstacles." Ganesha's domain is literature, and he dispenses much wisdom. Summon him for any new business and for rituals of prosperity. Many people keep Ganesha figures and images in their offices and on altars to ensure that he keeps obstacles at bay. Money spells and work-related rites are greatly abetted by the presence of this agreeable divinity.

Hermes: Revealer of Mysteries

He is associated with the Roman god Mercury and the Egyptian scribe god, Thoth. Hermes is an important deity for astrologers and metaphysicians, as he is credited with the invention of alchemy, astrology and several other occult sciences. "Thrice Great Hermes" is revered by ceremonial magicians, and is believed to be the wisest of all. He is the psychopomp who conducts the newly dead to the Underworld. Early Christians and Gnostics saw Hermes as a precursor to Christ, a divine prophet, the revealer of mysteries, and the giver of enlightenment. The Hermetic Cross is an adaptation of the insignia of Hermes. Hermes should be invoked if you are fashioning any rituals using the signs of the zodiac, foretelling the future or acquiring the deepest wisdom.

Horus: The Sun Is His Right Eye and the Moon is His Left

He is the Egyptian god of light and healing, the "all-seeing eye," and child of Isis and Osiris. Horus is often depicted with the head of a falcon and the body of a man. You can turn to him in meditation and prayer when you are looking for his beacon of "enlightenment." Horus is also a healing power to invoke in healing rituals.

Janus: The Gatekeeper of the Year

He is the gatekeeper from whom the word "janitor" comes. Janus has two faces, and was at one time identified with Jupiter. He is the gatekeeper of the year, as the divinity of the first month of the year, January.

Lugh: God of the Harvest

His name comes from the Celtic languages, translating to "Shining One." He is a warrior sun god and also guardian of the crops. Lugh has his own festival, Lughnasadh, which takes place every year on August 1 to celebrate harvest time. A ritual of gratitude for life, luck and prosperity will keep the bounty flowing. If you need a guardian or help with interpersonal problems at work, turn to Lugh as your defensive deity.

Mithra: Crowned By Cosmic Rays

He is the "Bringer of Light," a Persian god of the sun and protector of warriors. Mithra corresponds with the element of air and comes from a deep mystery tradition of Mesopotamian magic and fertility rites. If you have a loved one in a war far away from home, you should create a special altar for your beloved with Mithra, who is the "soldier's god."

Odin: Father of Wisdom

He is the Norse equivalent of Zeus and Jupiter, and is King of the Aesir. Odin rules wisdom, language, war and poetry. You can appeal to him by carving runes or writing poetry. Odin can help you with any kind of writing, giving you the energy to forge ahead with purpose and passion. He can even help you write your own rituals and poetic magical chants.

Osiris: Lunar Egyptian God of Beginnings and Endings

He is the Egyptian god of death and rebirth, who also takes care of the crops, the mind, the afterlife and manners. Husband to Isis and father of Horus, Osiris is a green god who is deeply connected to the cycles of growing and changing seasons. Turn to this god for rites of remembrance and for help with grief and mourning.

Pan: Bucolic Earth Deity

He is the goat-like god of the pastoral world, as well as of lust and fertility. Pan represents the earth element and can be invoked for any erotic spells or ceremonies of a sexual nature. Call on Pan any time you want to have fun. As a minor love god, he is an essential guest for Beltane, a modern Pagan version of Valentine's Day.

Talieisin: Wizard, Bard and Prophet

Although not technically a god, this monumental figure is said to live in the land or "summer stars" and is invoked in higher degrees of initiation in some esoteric orders. Talieisin is the harper poet from Welsh tradition, steeped in magic and mystery. He is associated with the magic of poetry, and embodies wisdom and clairvoyance. Talieisin is a helpmate to musicians and creative folks. If you are a solo practitioner and want to create a ceremony of self-initiation, Taliesin is a potent power to engage.

Thor: Power of Protection

The Norse sky and thunder god of justice and battle uses his thunderbolt to exact his will. Medieval Scandinavians believed the crack of lightning and thunder was Thor's chariot rolling through the heavens. Turn to Thor when you need spirituality to solve a legal matter. He is also a powerful protection deity to use in ritual.

Calling Down the Sisterhood: Invoking Goddesses in Your Spellwork

Below is a group of goddesses you can invoke and honor in your ritual work. I strongly advise placing images of a goddess on your altar when you need her aid, her strength, or her special qualities.

Aradia: Lunar Protectress

She is the Italian "Queen of the Witches" who descends to earth to preserve the magic of the goddess, Diana, her mother. Through Aradia's lineage, she is also a lunar deity. She is affiliated specifically with Dianic Wicca. Aradia is an excellent goddess to invoke for protection for any moon rituals you perform or create.

Artemis: Queen of the Moon

She is the Greek goddess of the moon. In her Roman form as Diana, she is the deity to whom Dianic witches and priestesses are devoted. She is a bringer of luck, the goddess of the hunt, and a powerful deity for magic and spell work. As the huntress, she can help you search out anything you are looking for, whether it is tangible or intangible. As a lunar deity, she can illuminate you. Invoke Artemis when you want to practice moon magic, and study her mythology further to design original lunar ceremonies. Enshrine her to bring good luck.

Athena: She Who Knows All

She is a goddess who rules both wisdom and war. Athena is a deity to invoke if you are doing ceremonies for peace, learning, protection, or any work-related issues. She can help you overcome any conflict with friends, families or foes.

Brigid: Guardian of Children and Animals

She was a Celtic solar goddess of poetry, smithcraft, and healing before the Catholic Church canonized her as a saint. Brigid is dually connected to the elements of water and fire. One way to bless water for ceremonies, your altar and home is to pray to Brigid to sanctify the water. She is a guardian for all animals and children, taking care of all matters related to child rearing. Brigid is also a goddess of inspiration. You can create creativity rituals or purification rites that include Brigid.

Ceres: Goddess of Plenty

She is the great Roman grain goddess. Think of her every time you have some cereal, which is named after her. The early summer festival, the Cerealia, honors Ceres for supplying the harvest and an abundance of crops. Any ceremony for planting, growing and cooking could involve this bounty-bringer. If you are going to plant a magical garden, craft a ritual with Ceres and make an outdoor altar to this grain goddess.

Hecate: The Face of the Dark Moon

She is a crone goddess who shows her face in the dark moon. Hecate is the goddess of where three paths meet and as the banisher of evil, which serves us well in rites of closure, "letting go," and getting rid of any negatively charged aspect of your life. Any time you want to bring something to an end, invoke Hecate for help. Funeral rites or ceremonies of remembrance, especially those for older women, are appropriate occasions for summoning Hecate.

As the personification of the dark moon, she is also the goddess of divination and prophecy. Try creating a dark moon prophecy circle, and invite her for deep and wise insight. Design a ritual during the dark moon with Hecate for ultimate feminine wisdom and a fresh new beginning.

Hestia: Ruler of Hearth and Home

She is the goddess of home and hearth whom the Romans knew as Vesta. Hestia is associated with the element of fire, and is concerned with the safety and security of the individual as well as families. As goddess of the hearth, she rules the kitchen, making it possible to perform magical baking recipes with your mixing bowl serving as a cauldron, enchanting it with spices such as cinnamon and cloves. Hestia is the perfect deity to help design a new house. She is a blessing there to help you with cleaning and purification rituals in your living space and sacred space.

Hokmah: She of the Highest Wisdom

She is the holy spirit, an ancient Hebrew goddess of wisdom, the Gnostic Sophia. Hokmah is also related to Egypt's Ma'at, mother of creative works of power, from which the universe was formed. It was believed by scholars that *bereshith*, the very first word of Genesis, really refers to this goddess of wisdom. The book *Targum of Jerusalem* discusses the first words of Genesis and the goddess of wisdom at length. *Bereshith* is traditionally translated as "in the beginning." Hokmah appears often in pre-Christian and early Christian writings, and Philo of Alexandria described her as the spouse of Jehovah. King Solomon himself decreed that Hokmah must be obeyed in "The Wisdom of Solomon," a chapter not included in the biblical canon and established as apocryphal. Hokmah's symbol, like that of Venus, is the dove. You can summon the eternal wisdom of Hokmah with an image of a dove on your altar. Ignored and redacted from history, she holds vast beneficial power. You can design a women's mystery rite by meditating on this ancient spirit. Allow inspiration to come and be literally filled with the holy spirit. Her wisdom will enlighten you and reveal how the rite should be designed.

Isis: The Queen of Heaven

Isis is the only goddess who could guarantee the immortality of the Egyptian pharaohs, resurrecting them as she did Osiris. Her worship spread, becoming an enormous cult that appealed to the entire Roman Empire. She has great appeal as a divine mother. Isis is the daughter of Nuit, the goddess of the sky, and of Seb, the god of earth. The ancients worshipped her as the Queen of Heaven, and she is often depicted with wings.

Isis is the link between birth and death and can be invoked in rituals designed to celebrate existence under our banner of stars. Her origins in myth show her to have begun as a sun deity, but her sphere of influence has grown to include the moon.

Kali: Mother of All Creation

She is the Hindu goddess of the ever-cycling nature of creation and destruction. Kali can be called on to protect and defend women of any age. If you are afraid for yourself, pray aloud to Kali in her destroyer aspect, which wears a necklace of skulls that will scare off any attacker. If someone is recovering from an abusive relationship, Kali can be called on to help with healing and renewing courage and self-esteem. Kali is not to be feared, but respected and admired. One of Kali's aspects is the Indian goddess, Vac. This incarnation of Kali is the "Mother of All Creation" who spoke the first word, *OM*, which gave birth to the universe. She also invented the Sanskrit alphabet. An image of Kali in your office or cubicle will keep trouble at bay and keep you strong and active and fully in your power. Give offerings to her occasionally with your girlfriends in your life with "womanpower" rituals.

Selene: The Teacher of Magic

She is the full moon, another Greek aspect of the lunation cycle. She sheds light on the world and on all of us, inside and out. Her mythology is that as a teacher of magic and all things supernatural, passing her special knowledge on to her students. She is also a mentor, and her light illuminates our intelligence and ability to think clearly with logic.

Shekina: The Splendor That Feeds Angels

She is the female deity who is "God's glory" and the spouse of an ancient Hebrew god. Older rabbinical texts describe her as the "splendor that feeds angels." She was the only one to get away with being angry with the Hebrew god. She is associated with Sophia and Mari-Anna. Having been redacted from all biblical texts, Shekina was veiled in obscurity until some medieval cabbalists rediscovered her. Glimmerings of Shekina show up in passages of the Talmud, telling the story of the exiled Israelis wandering into the wilderness with Joseph's bones and a second ossuary, or "bone box," containing "the Shekina" in the form of a pair of stone tablets. Be very creative in designing rituals, altars, offerings and ceremonies honoring this deity, since you are rebuilding a lost part of goddess history. One daring ritual could include calling a women's circle and rewriting the tablets of wisdom. Call upon your inner Shekina and inner knowledge for guidance in this highly original approach to ritual.

Sige: The Primordial Female Creator

This Gnostic goddess charges us to be silent. In Roman mythology she stands for the secret name of Rome, which could not be spoken aloud, and thus she is depicted as a hooded woman with a finger to her lips. Gnostic texts speak of Sige's origins as the mother of Sophia. She is the primordial female creator: out of silence came the *logos,* or the word. The cult, rituals and folklore regarding Sige were held so strictly secret that we know nothing about them now. But, since creation comes out of silence, there is complete creative freedom for you to recreate new myths, stories and celebrations for this obscure deity. Silent celebrations, quiet meditations and secret spells no doubt have the approval of Sige.

Sunna: Shedding Light on the World

She is the ancient Germanic goddess of the sun, proof that our big star is not always deified as male. The Teutons also referred to this very important divine entity as "Glory of Elves." In the great Northern European saga, the *Poetic Edda*, Sunna was said to have a daughter who sheds light on a brand-new world. Other sun goddesses include the Arabian Attar, the Japanese Amarterasu and the British Sulis, "the sun's eye."

Venus: Daughter of the Moon

The Roman goddess of love, Venus is associated with ultimate femininity, ultimate sexuality, ultimate fertility and all that is beautiful. In Western early myth, the planet Venus was seen as "Daughter of the Moon" and all of the early Venusian goddesses have Neolithic roots as lunar deities. The word *veneration* means to worship Venus, and she should be venerated in all the love spells of your own design as well as celebrations and circles taking place on her day—Friday. The lore and mythology of Venus is well known, as she has been imprinted on our consciousness as the beautiful naked nymph on a half shell rising out of a foamy wave of the ocean. Honor her by creating venerable dances on the beach, and write love prayers and poems inspired by the love in your own heart.

Deities of the Ancients

Supreme God: Woden, Frigg (Germanic); Jupiter, Juno (Roman); Zeus, Hera (Greek); Ra (Egyptian); Marduk (Babylonian)

Creator: Ptah (Egyptian); Anu (Babylonian)

Sky: Frigg (Germanic); Jupiter (Roman); Uranus, Zeus (Greek); Nut (Egyptian); Anu (Babylonian)

Sun: Apollo (Roman); Helios (Greek); Ra (Egyptian); Anu, Anshar (Babylonian)

Moon: Diana (Roman); Artemis (Greek); Thoth (Egyptian); Sin (Babylonian)

Earth: Sif (Germanic); Tellus (Roman); Gaia (Greek); Geb (Egyptian); Enlil (Babylonian)

Air: Enlil (Babylonian)

Fire: Hoenir (Germanic); Vulcan (Roman); Hephaestus (Greek); Girru (Babylonian)

Sea: Niord (Germanic); Neptune (Roman); Poseidon (Greek)

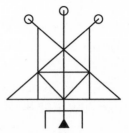

Chapter 10:

Rites of Passage: Rituals and Invocations for Groups and Gatherings

S abbats are the holy days for each season of the year in accordance with the celestial spheres above. Some of these holy days celebrate the arrival of spring and the start of new growth, and others mark harvest in preparation for the dark and chilly days of winter. Nearly all our festivals have roots in the ancient rites based on fertility and the hopes of abundant farm crops.

Humankind first marked time by the movement of the stars, sun and moon in the sky, which also informed the designation of constellations and astrological calendars. Candlemas, Beltane, Lammas Day and All Hallow's Eve are the major sabbats. The lesser sabbats, listed below, are the astrological markers of new seasons:

Celestial Celebrations and Lunar Festivals

Ostara: March 21; is also known as the Vernal or Spring Equinox

Lithe: June 21; is commonly known as the Summer Solstice

Macon: September 21; is best known as the Autumnal Equinox

Yule: December 21; is the Winter Solstice

Full Moon: Calling Forth Your Personal Power

When the moon is full, that means Mother Moon is at her zenith, parading in all her glory across the night sky. Rituals that transform and call forth your personal power and psychic awareness are called for at this time. The full moon is powerful and promotes strength and supremacy. Her luminous glow surrounds us, and now is the time to clean our ritual tools, scrying mirrors, tarot decks and crystals. Take time to honor the moon goddess during this phase. Wiccans have a tradition of "drawing down the moon," which is a way of invoking the moon's power into your body, thereby embodying the lunar goddess.

Although many cultures around the world have had ceremonies to celebrate the full moon, only a few are still practiced today. The Balinese have received wide interest for their full moon ritual, and Bali has become a popular destination for people on a pilgrimage who want to be in touch with the sacred. A growing number of nature-worshiping people gather in magical circles to do the same in North America and Europe.

In Peru there is a sacred site, the Quenko-Labyrinth of the Serpent, where full moon ceremonies are held. It is believed that on this site you can experience your true connection with the earth, the feminine and life, for this sacred site embodies the Goddess. Rites of passage and sacred ritual offerings have been performed here for centuries. Shamans teach this as an important way for humankind to connect with and balance nature and community.

Lunar Eclipse Rite: That Which is Hidden Will Be Revealed

Astrologers and wise elders will tell you that major events happen in the world during the eclipse time; secrets are revealed, scandals occur, stock markets drop and all manners surprise. During these rare celestial occurrences, that which has been hidden shall be revealed. Vikings and their brethren believed the sun and moon were created by benevolent gods to bring light to a dark world. The Norse gods placed the sun and the moon in chariots that flew across the sky, shedding light on the entire world. However, the hungry giant wolf chased the sun and, every once in a while, caught up with it and devoured it, which darkened the sky. When the sun began to burn the insides of the wolf, he would cough it back into the sky. This, according to Nordic folklore, is how eclipses happen.

Eclipses are celestial events that still fascinate us, and you can easily gather a group together for a ritual. Invite enough people to form two circles. Twenty is ideal, so you have ten in each circle. Ask half of the people to wear all gold and the other half to wear all black. Those in black are the Sky Wolves who will eat the sun, represented by those in gold. For safety, everyone needs to wear their best UV protection sunglasses (in gray, brown, or green) to safeguard their eyes.

Well in advance of the eclipse, form the circles and tell the story of the Fenris Wolf. Ask other people if they have any experiences of past eclipses they can share with the group. Ten minutes before the eclipse begins, have the gold group form a circle around the black group. Direct the two circles to walk, dance or move in opposite directions. Five minutes before the eclipse begins, have the black group move outside the gold circle and have the gold circle sit down.

I have witnessed people barking, howling and moaning to express their roles and the immense power of this imminent heavenly happening. During the actual event, however, everyone will grow silent and experience the extraordinary power of this rare and sacred heavenly moment. As always, people should only look at the sun through special filters. The best way to experience this ritual is to sit with eyes closed and *feel* its immensity.

In about ten minutes, as the eclipse is occurring, the black-garbed folks should walk away one by one at least ten feet and sit in a circle. When the gold circle is the only group left, the symbolism is the full reappearance of the sun.

When people begin to stir and want to talk, ask everyone to share what came to mind. People often have amazing insights and visions during eclipses. Document these "eclipse epiphanies," if possible, and remember to include them in your storytelling for the next eclipse ritual.

One Moon for All the World: New Year's Council Fire

Any discussion of rituals for the month of January must include New Year's Eve and New Year's Day. I remember the drama that ensued as people around the globe stood by to witness the sunrise on January 1, 2000, perceived as the beginning of the new millennium. While many other cultures observe their New Year at other times during the year, January 1 has also become a time of celebration, reflection and an opportunity to embrace change.

For many millennia, indigenous peoples have celebrated their own New Year in unique ways. One common element is the use of fire rituals by North, Central, and South American peoples. The Pilgrims who arrived to what was to become New England observed and documented that the Iroquois and other tribes they encountered had a New Year's Council Fire, a time when the tribe gathered to review the past year, listen to their elders and speak their hopes, dreams, and visions of the coming year. In addition to your personal New Year's ritual with the significant people in your life, I recommend a Bonfire Ceremony as a powerful way to bring positive change of the New Year into your life.

Bonfire Ceremonies are considered to open a door or portal into the spirit world that held the promise of receiving the blessings of spirit-love, healing, prosperity, peace and anything you need for personal transformation. This ritual is also an opportunity to pay respects and make homage to your ancestors and loved ones you have lost. For this reason alone, I suggest enacting the Fire Ceremony: our culture is losing the important connection to the older people in our lives. Involving them in the rituals, ceremonies and passages of our lives could heal a cultural rift and bring deep wisdom to all. Mayan shamans could "read" the fire in a divinatory fashion, and I hear that some modern metaphysicians can do the same. If you are fortunate enough to know anyone with such skills, invite them to your fire ceremony to share what they divine from the flames.

Sabbat of Imbolc: A February Festival

Although February is the shortest calendar month, it holds many rich festivals from several cultures. Celtic Pagans celebrate Imbolc, or Brigid's Day, as the first sign of spring in the Wheel of the Year.

Imbolc translates to "in the milk," which reflects the lambing and calving season that begins around this time. The idea of purification also runs through February festivals such as Purim, Candlemas and Lupercalia. Take the opportunity to start "spring cleaning" a bit earlier than you usually do to help chase away the winter blues. And of course, February holds Valentine's Day, a now-secular celebration of affection and friendship.

Imbolc Invocation: Calling Forth the Guardians

Candlemas, also known as Imbolc, is the highest point between the winter solstice and spring equinox. This festival anticipates the coming of spring with banquets and blessings. Tradition holds that milk must be served, and modern pagans have expanded that to butter cookies, ice cream, cheeses and any related foods. It is an important time to welcome new members of your spiritual circle and new witches into a coven. Candlemas is a heartwarming occasion, but it is still a wintry time, so kindling for the hearth or bonfire should include cedar, pine, juniper and holly along with wreaths of the same to mark the four directions alongside white candles in glass votives. Strong incense such as cedar, nag champa or frankincense will bless the space. The circle leader shall begin the ritual by lighting incense from the fire and begin by facing each direction, saying:

Welcome Guardians of the East, bringing your fresh winds and breath of life. Come to the circle of Imbolc.

Welcome Guardians of South, you bring us heart and health. Come to the circle on this Holy Day.

Welcome Guardian's of the West, place of setting sun and mighty mountains. Come to us.

Welcome Guardians of the North, land of life-giving rains and snow. Come to our circle on this sacred day.

The leader should welcome each member of the circle and speak to the gifts they bring to the community. Everyone should acknowledge each other with toasts and blessings and break bread together in this time of the coming season.

The First New Moon of the Year: Chinese New Year

This most special holiday for Chinese all over the world is a "moveable feast," as it occurs on the second new moon after the shortest day of the year (the winter solstice, December 21) and lasts about two weeks. According to the Western calendar, this means the holiday begins sometime in either late January or early February. Tradition holds that homes must be cleaned from top to bottom in preparation for the festivities. On New Year's Eve, families get together for a banquet, and at this feast fish is the dish of delight, as the Chinese word for "fish" sounds like *yu*, or "great plenty." Red is the color of luck and all children receive red envelopes filled with money and bright, shining moon-like coins. Adults write "spring couplets" on red paper; these are short poems that are hung around the doorway to greet the New Year auspiciously. Oranges are placed around the house in bowls and plates and blooming plants adorn the home both indoors and out. All generations of the extended Chinese family, from great-grandmother to the tiniest toddler, stay up late playing games, telling stories and making wishes for the New Year. They call this most auspicious time of the year "Hong

Bau," and apply the ancient and sacred principles of feng shui in a celebration of love and luck. Gather red envelopes, coins and paper money. The Chinese call the red envelopes *lee sees.*

On the actual day of the Chinese New Year, go around to your neighbors, friends and family with red envelopes containing money. If you are like me, bright, shiny coins are what you can easily afford to give instead of envelopes stuffed with paper money. With each gift, greet folks with *Gung Hey Fat Choy,* which means "Wishing you prosperity and health."

Give every child two *lee sees,* because happiness comes in pairs. By taking care to provide the children you know with *lee sees,* you are making sure the next generation has good luck. Business owners also give *lee sees* to employees, important partners and associates. When you hand a *lee see* to anyone you may have a grudge or grievance with, you should let go of the old feeling and refuse to drag the new you down with emotional baggage in the New Year.

Spring Seasonal Festivals

In March we see the more tangible signs of spring—grass and trees begin to green, birds return from where they have wintered, and we breathe in the warmer breezes that herald summer ahead. Be careful, however—March can be a month of surprises and changes. Celebrate spring by bringing fresh flowers into your home, and take advantage of the first fruits and vegetables in the markets. March marks the vernal (or spring) equinox, one of only two days of the year where the hours of daylight and the night are balanced equally. The vernal equinox, like its partner, the autumnal equinox, exemplifies the concept of equilibrium and the idea that two halves create a whole: only with the darkness can light be seen and appreciated.

Vernal Equinox: a Rite of Spring

At this time, celebrate the festival of Ostara, the Saxon goddess who is the personification of the rising sun. Ostara is derived from the Anglo-Saxon Eostre or Oestre, and her totem is the rabbit. Legend has it that her rabbit brought forth the brightly colored eggs now associated with Easter. At this time the world is warming under the sun as spring approaches. Every plant, animal, man and woman feels this growing fever for spring.

This ritual is intended for communities, so gather a group. Tell everyone to bring a "spring food" such as deviled eggs, salads with flowers in them, fresh broths, berries, mushrooms, fruits, pies, veggie casseroles or quiches. Have the food table at the opposite side of the gathering area away from the altar, but decorate it with flowers and pussy willow branches that are just beginning to bud. These are the harbingers of spring.

Essential elements for this ritual are an altar table; bay laurel leaves; bowls of water; multihued crystals; candles; a jar of honey; fruits of yellow, red, white and purple; musical instruments; and one bowl each of seeds, leaves, flowers and fruit.

Create your own Eostre altar in the middle of the ritual area by covering the table with a cloth of color that represents spring to you. It could be a richly hued flowered cloth or a light green solid color. The cloth should represent new life. Scatter Bay laurel leaves around the table. Place goddesses on the altar table, too, with

Eostre at the center. Put colored eggs, chocolate rabbits, candles and crystals around the goddesses. In the east, set a yellow candle and crystals of amber, gold and yellow, such as citrine or agate. Place yellow fruit, such as pears or bananas, in front of the candle as an offering to the energies of the east. In the south, set a red candle and red and orange stones, such as garnet or the newly available "rough rubies," which cost only a few cents each. Apples and pomegranates are excellent red food to place in front of the candle. In the west, set a purple candle with amethysts in front of it. Sweet plums are a perfect fruit to place in front of the candle. In the north, set a white candle and a clear quartz or white crystal. Honeydew melon is an appropriate selection for the fruit offering. Choose four representatives to invoke the directions.

East – Everyone faces east. The representative for the direction should weave a story and create a vision that can be shared by all that is characterized by new beginnings, such as the rising of the morning sun. Spring is the time for new beginnings and growth in nature. The speaker can, for example, take the bowl of seeds and tell the tale of the seeds sprouting in the dark moist soil of Mother Earth. Pass the bowl of seeds around to everyone and urge them to take some seeds home to plant.

South – Everyone faces south. The speaker for this direction should invoke the power of the leaf. Leaves draw in the energy of the sun through photosynthesis and help keep an important cycle of life moving. Leaves grow throughout the summer season, drinking in the water of life and using the power of the sun for photosynthesis. Pass the bowl of leaves around the group.

West – Everyone faces west. The speaker for this direction should invoke the power of flowers. Flowers bud and bloom. They follow the sun and are some of nature's purest expressions of beauty. Flowers bring joy to people, and many flowers become fruit. Pass the bowl of flowers to the group and urge everyone to take some.

North – Everyone faces the north. The speaker for the north should invoke fruit and harvest time. Fruit is the result of nature's generosity. Fruit also contains the seeds for our future. Pass the bowl of fruit around and suggest everyone take one and eat it, meditating on the glory and deep meaning it contains. If it is appropriate, you can also offer juice or wine as part of the fruit invocation. Wine is the glorious nectar of fruit.

Now it's time for the ritual enactment. Everyone takes a seat around the altar. Drummers should start to play a gentle rhythm. Chanting, singing and ululating are also encouraged, however people feel comfortable expressing themselves.

Each speaker should in turn light a candle and invoke the ancestors of the group. Special time should be given for remembrances to people who have died in the past year and are an important respect paid to the community at large.

Next is the honoring of the moon. Ask people to speak about the moon, reciting their favorite moon poems or moon memories.

Anointing the third eye blesses your insight for the coming year. Pass the bowls of water and laurel leaves around. Take a leaf and dip it in the water, then touch the wet leaf to your third eye. Pass the bowl on to the next person. When the bowl has made its way back to the ritual leader, sing and dance in celebration of spring. Everyone should get in a line and hold hands and dance around the circle, like a plant moving and growing, flowering and fruiting.

When the four speakers feel that the energy has reached a climax, each one should clap and say in turn:

And now it is done; now it is spring!

They open the circle by saying together:

It is spring in the East, it is spring in the South, it is spring in the West, and it is spring in the North!

Let the Good Times Roll: Mardi Gras Moveable Feast

Mardi Gras means "Fat Tuesday," the last day before Lent, when Catholics were formerly forbidden to eat meat (or fat). Fat Tuesday is the day before Ash Wednesday, when the Lenten season begins. Depending on how early or late Easter is each year, Mardi Gras, or Carnival, can be celebrated in March or April. The first Mardi Gras celebration was in New Orleans in 1827. In olden times, people dressed in animal skin, pelted each other with bunches of flowers and drank wine. Also called Carnival, this is a very important rite of spring and has traveled all over the world. It is perhaps most grandly celebrated in Brazil. Carnival and Mardi Gras last for days and involve parades, costumes, special foods and much frolicking. This is an opportunity for you to choose what most appeals to you and create a gorgeous spring ritual.

Beltane Eve, April 30

Beltane is without a doubt the sexiest of pagan High Holidays and is anticipated greatly throughout the year. Witchy ones celebrate this holy night which falls on the last eve of April, and it is traditional for celebrations to last the entire night. This is a festival for feasting, singing, laughter and lovemaking. On May Day, when the sun returns in the morning, revelers gather to erect a merrily beribboned Maypole to dance around, followed by picnicking and sensual siestas. The recipe below is befitting for this special time of the year when love flows as freely as wine.

Sharing the Love: DIY Beltane Brew

Honeyed mead is revered as the drink of choice for this sexiest of pagan holy days. It is an aphrodisiac and signals the ripeness of this day devoted to love and lust. This recipe is adapted from a medieval method.

- 1 quart honey

- 1 packet of yeast

- 3 quarts distilled water

- Herbs to flavor such as cinnamon, nutmeg or vanilla, according to your preference

Step 1: Mix the honey and water. Boil for five minutes. You can add the herbs to your liking but I prefer a tablespoon each of clove, nutmeg, cinnamon, and all-spice.

Step 2: Add a packet of yeast and mix. Put in a large container. Cover with plastic wrap and allow to rise and expand. Store the mix in a dark place and allow it to set for seven days, ideally at the beginning of a new moon phase.

Step 3: Refrigerate for three days while the sediment settles at the bottom. Strain and store in a colored glass bottle, preferably green. You can drink it now, but after seven months, it has gained a full-bodied flavor. Always keep in a cool dark place.

Nonalcoholic Mead

- 1 quart honey

- 3 quarts distilled water

- ½ cup lemon juice

- 1 sliced lemon

- 1 half teaspoon nutmeg

- 1 pinch of salt

Boil all the mixed ingredients for five minutes and let cool. Bottle immediately in a colored glass jar. Keep this in the fridge to avoid fermentation and enjoy any festive occasion. This is a healthy and refreshing way to celebrate.

A Toast To Love: Hoof and Horn Rite

Ideally, celebrate outdoors, but if indoor-bound on Beltane Eve, pick a place with a fireplace and have a roaring blaze so celebrants can wear comfy clothing and dance barefoot. Ask them to bring spring flowers and musical instruments, plenty of drums! Place pillows on the floor and serve an ambrosial spread of finger foods, honeyed mead, beer, spiced cider, wine and fruity teas. As you light circle incense, set out green, red and white candles, one for each participant. When it is time to call the circle, raise your arm and point to each direction, saying "To the East, to the North," etc., then sing:

Hoof and horn, hoof and horn, tonight our spirits are reborn. (Repeat thrice)

Welcome, joy, to this home. Fill these friends with love and laughter. So mote it be.

Have each guest light a candle and speak to the subject of love with a toast of Beltane Brew. Drumming and dancing is the next part of the circle. This is truly an invocation of lust for life and will be a night to remember for all. Now rejoice!

Summers of Love and Joy

Blessings From the East: Prayer to Honor the Summer

For summer festivals such as the Summer Solstice on June 21, you should honor the deities who gift us with such plenty. Light yellow and green candles at your altar and on the feast table and offer this appeal:

Oh, Lady of Summer
Who brings and sun and life-giving rains,
May each harvest bring the crops that fill our cups.
The rivers and oceans, fields and farms are yours.
We honor you today and give thanks to you for all we have.
A toast to thee, blessed be!

Sacred Grove Solstice Spell – June 21

Celebrating the season of the sun is best done outdoors in the glory of nature's full bloom. If you have a forest nearby or a favorite grove of trees, plan to picnic and share this rite of passage with your spiritual circle. Covens often have a favorite spot. All the better if a great oak is growing there, the tree most sacred to Druids. Gather the tribe and bring brightly colored ribbons and indelible markers. Form the circle by holding hands, then point to east, south, north and west chanting:

We hold the wisdom of the sun,
We see the beauty of our earth.
To the universe that gives us life, we return the gift.
Deepest peace to all,
And we are all one. Blessed be.

Each member of the circle should speak their wish for the world, themselves or loved ones and write it on a ribbon. One by one, tie your ribbon to a tree. Each flutter of the wind will spread your well-wishes.

Lammas Day, August 2 – Harvesting Happiness

This major sabbat denotes the high point of the year; the crops are in their fullness, weather is warm and the countryside is bursting forth with the beauty of life. Pagans know we have the heavens above to thank for this and the gods of nature must be acknowledged for their generosity with a gathering of the tribe and a feast, ideally in the great outdoors. Ask invitees to bring harvest-themed offerings for the altar: gourds, pumpkins, bundles of wheat stalks and corn, or fresh pickings from their garden, and food to share in thanksgiving made from the same, like pies, tomato salads, cucumber pickles, green beans, corn pudding, watermelon, lemon cakes, berry cucumber, apple cider and beer brewed from wheat, hops and barley. This celebration of the reaping from summer season should reflect what you have grown with your own hands. Fill your cauldron or a big beautiful colored glass bowl half-full with freshly-drawn water. Get packets of tiny votive candles for floating in the water. At the feast table, make sure to have a place-setting for the godly guest Lugh who watched over the plantings to ensure this bounty. Place loaves of Lammas bread by his plate.

When all guests have arrived, everyone should add a food offering to the plate of the god and light a candle to float in the cauldron. Cut a slice of Lammas bread for Lugh and begin the ceremony with this prayer of thanks:

Oh, ancient Lugh of the fields and farms,
We invite you here with open arms,
In this place between worlds, in flowering fields of hay.
You have brought the blessings we receive this Lammas Day.

Begin the feast and before the dessert course, everyone should go around the table and speak to their gratitude for the gifts of the year. Storytelling, singing, spiral dances and all manner of merriment is part of Lammas Day.

Indonesian Full Moon Ceremony

Nearly every temple in Bali celebrates this monthly event.

Essential elements for this ritual are incense, offerings of fruit and lots of flowers, rice, and holy or blessed water.

Gather a group of like-minded folks and head to the nearest body of water—a lake, pond, creek, river or the ocean. Nature will be your temple.

Begin by sitting in a circle and making garlands of flowers. You should talk, laugh or be silent as you wish, but most important, be comfortable. When everyone is settled with a garland of flowers, place the garland around the neck of another person. Light the incense and set the rice and holy water in the middle of the circle.

Go around the circle and offer the water to people, sprinkling it on them gently with your fingertips in the Balinese fashion, and offer everyone a cupful of the holy water to rinse their mouths with so the worst they speak will be holier. Each person should make a fruit or flower offering to the gods, and lay it near the cleansing smoke of incense. After the offerings are made, everyone should anoint their neighbor's forehead with grains of rice and speak blessings aloud for each person. If a body of water is accessible, get wet, even if it is just to dip your hands or walk in the water.

Silently acknowledge the blessings in your life through prayer and meditation, and, again, give quiet thanks to the gods for the gift of your life. Unlike most Western-based rituals, there is not much talking during the Balinese Full Moon Ritual. Bask in the tranquility and listen to your thoughts.

Autumnal Equinox Ritual: Macon, September 21

Establish one room in your house as the temple. Ideally, it is the room in which you normally keep an altar or sacred shrine. In any case, you should create an altar in the center of the space. Place four small tables in the four corners of the directions and place four evenly spaced candlesticks between the tables. Place a loaf of freshly baked bread (bread you have made with your own hands is best) in the east, a bowl of apples in the south, a bottle of wine in the west, and a sheaf of wheat or a bundle of dried corn in the north. Upon the main altar, place a candle, a plate of sweet cakes and a goblet. Light incense and place it in front of the cakes. Before your ritual, take some time for contemplation. Think about what you have achieved during this busy year:

What have you done?

What do you need?

What remains to be done?

What are your aspirations?

Write down your thoughts and feelings and the answers to those questions. Read what you have written and ponder it. Look for continuing ideas or themes and make notes of these on a piece of paper. Light the candle on the altar and use this candle to light all the other candles in the temple.

Now go around your temple space in reverse order and extinguish all candles. Then declare your temple closed. The common wisdom is that you should place the apples, bread and wine in your garden as an offering the next day, as a blessing to all of nature.

Sabbat of Samhain – October 31st All Hallow's Eve

Halloween stems from the grand tradition of the Celtic New Year. What started as a folk festival celebrated by small groups in rural areas has come to be the second largest holiday of today. There are multitudinous reasons—including modern marketing—but I think it satisfies a basic human need, to let your "wild side" out, to be free and more connected with the ancient ways. This is the time when the veil between worlds is thinnest and you can commune with the other side, with elders and the spirit world. It is important to honor the ancestors during this major sabbat and acknowledge what transpired in the passing year as well as set intentions for the coming year.

This is the ideal time to invite your circle; the ideal number for your gathering is thirteen. Gather powdered incense, salt, a loaf of bread, goblets for wine and three candles to represent the triple goddess for altar offerings. Ideally on an outdoor stone altar, pour the powdered incense into a pentagram star shape. Let go of old sorrows, angers and anything not befitting of new beginnings in this New Year. Bring only your best to this auspicious occasion.

Light the candles and say:

In honor of the Triple Goddess on this sacred night of Samhain,
All the ancient ones
From time before time
To those behind the veil.

Rap the altar three times and light the incense. Say this blessing aloud:

198

For this bread, wine, and salt,
We ask the blessings of Mother, Maiden and Crone,
And the gods who guard the Gate of the World.

Sprinkle salt over the bread, eat the bread and drink the wine.

Each of the celebrants should come to the altar repeating the bread and wine blessing. After this, be seated and everyone in turn should name those on the other side and offer thanks to ancestors and deities. This can and should take a long time as we owe much to loved ones on the other side.

Winter Is Coming Solstice Circle

December 21 - Longest Night Fire Ceremony

December is named for the Roman goddess Decima, one of the three fates. The word Yule comes from the Germanic *jol*, which means midwinter, and is celebrated on the shortest day of the year. The old tradition was to have a vigil at a bonfire to make sure the sun did indeed rise again. This primeval custom evolved to become a storytelling evening and while it may well to be too cold to sit outside in snow and sleet, congregating around a blazing hearth fire, dining and talking deep into the night is important for your community to truly know each other, impart wisdom and speak to hopes and dreams. Greet the new sun with stronger connections and a shared vision for the coming solar year.

What you need:

- Candles in the following colors: red, yellow, green, blue, white and black

- Herbs: tobacco, rosemary, lavender, cedar, sage, and rose petals

- Incense: copal, myrrh, or any resin-based incense

- 2 cups sugar

- 1 chocolate bar per person

- Bells, rattles, drus, and other noisemakers

- A firepot, fireplace, or safe place for an outdoor fire

- Paper for written intentions

The candle colors represent the six directions: north, south, east, west, up, and down (or sky and earth). They also represent the different people of the world.

Gather your friends together at dusk on the shortest day of the year and ask them to bring a colored candle (assign them a color), a noisemaker, and an open mind. Ask them also to write out what they want to purge from their life and bring the paper into the circle. The Solstice Fire Ceremony serves to bring positive new influences into our lives and also to dispel what no longer serves for good. This "letting go" can be anything. For me, one year ago, it was cancer, and this year it was too much clutter. For you, it could be an unhealthy relationship, a job that makes you miserable, or a cramped apartment.

Here are the steps to the ritual:

Build a fire at 5:00 p.m. and have it burning brightly as your guests arrive. Place a big bowl of herbs, flower petals, and incense near the fire.

Create a circle around the fire and ask the eldest in the group to slowly draw a circle of sugar around the fire.

When the elder has moved back into place in the circle, each person should light his or her candles from the fire and place it in the sugar circle, creating a mandala.

Ask the youngest person to lead the group in this chant:

My life is my own
I must but choose to be better,
Vital breath of life I breathe
No more pain and strife!
Wise ones, bring us health and life
Bring us love and luck
Bring us blessed peace
On this Winter's Day.
Into the fire, we toss the old
Into the fire, we see our future
On this, our longest night.
Harm to none and health to all!

Everyone should rattle and drum away, making merry and rousing the good spirits. The spirits of the wise elders will join you.

After the drumming, start around the circle, beginning with the eldest. Allow people to speak about what they want to release from their life, and have them toss their "letting go" paper into the fire. Then the eldest person should lead the group in a prayer for collective hopes for the coming your, and anyone who wants to add something should also speak out wishes for positive change, for themselves and for the world.

Thank the wise elders and ancestors for their wisdom and spiritual aid by throwing some chocolate into the fire. Be sure to keep some for members of the circle to share and enjoy. The Mayans held the belief that a plentitude of offerings to the ancestors would bring more blessings. They also believed that fire ceremonies helped support the planet and all the nations of the word. Gifts to the fire signal to the elders that they can return through the door and to the other world, until you call upon them for help in the future.

Lunar Astrology is the calendar by which early humans marked the passing of time and how they evolved their calendar, which is a lunar calendar. You should keep track of the moon and see what works for you.

Astrological Almanac: Moon Signs of the Times

The astrological signs of the moon are of great significance. Each moon sign has special meaning set down through the centuries. Ancient and medieval folks paid strict attention to moon phases and moon signs for planting and harvesting. Here is a guide to each sign with tried and true lore from olden days along with applications for today's rituals.

Aries is a barren and dry sign that is perfect for planting, weeding, haying and harvesting. Moon in Aries is the optimum time for rituals pertaining to leadership, pioneering, ambition and authority, as well as rebirth. Any healing regarding the face and head is more successful during Aries.

Taurus is an earthy and moist sign that is excellent for planting root crops like potatoes and peanuts. Love, money and luxury are the watchwords for moon in Taurus. If you are buying real estate, moon in Taurus is an excellent time for that. Because the throat and neck are ruled by Taurus, this is a prime time both for singing and speaking.

Gemini is another dry sign that is best time for mowing, cutting and getting rid of plants or pests. Communication is improved during moon in Gemini. Healing for the arms and hands and pulmonary system is well advised during a Gemini moon.

Cancer is a fruitful watery sign conductive to planting; in fact, it is the most productive sign of all. Hearth and home are the focus now and lunar rituals are well timed during moon in Cancer. Healing rituals for the stomach are done best at this time.

Leo is the driest and least fertile of all moon signs, good only for cutting and mowing. Leo moon is good for bravery, striking out in a new direction, like performing on stage or taking a position of authority. Matters of the heart and literal healing of the organ are advisable now.

Virgo is both damp and barren, but is a great time for cultivation. Virgo moon is good for working hard and seeking employment, tending to all aspects of health, nutrition and healing the nervous system and bowel.

Libra is both wet and fruitful and is wonderful for grains, vines, root crops and flowers. Now is the time for artistic endeavors, romantic liaisons and balancing your life. The lower back and kidneys can be restored to health during moon in Libra.

Scorpio is humid and bountiful and is good for all types of planting. Make your moves during moon in Scorpio. This sign is also conducive to plumbing the depths of the spirit and achieving psychic growth. Sex rituals are at their most potent during moon in Scorpio. Healing of the sensitive reproductive organs can happen during this moon time.

Sagittarius is another fire sign that is a poor time for planting and is best spent harvesting and storing. Rites of passage and travel and rituals relating to higher truths and philosophical matters succeed during moon in Sagittarius. Sports and horses are also in the spotlight during this time. Healing for the legs can be undertaken during this time.

Capricorn is an earth sign that is also wet and is excellent for grafting, pruning and planting trees and shrubs. Rituals relating to work, goals, and organizing can be commenced at this time. Political careers, dreams and aspirations should be launched during moon in Capricorn. Skeletal wellness is advisable during this cycle as well.

Aquarius is an infertile and parched moon time that is best for harvesting, weeding and dispelling pests. The Aquarian moon is appropriate for rites regarding personal freedom. Friendship, the intellect and starting a new phase of life all come into play now. Rituals of a more radical nature are best during this sign. Shin and ankle health goes better now, too.

Pisces is fecund and fruitful and is good for all kinds of planting. It is remarkable for fruits of all kinds. The highly sensitive moon in Pisces is good for spells and charms for creativity, intuition, divination, dream work and music. Care and healing for the feet is most favorable during this sign of moon in Pisces.

Power of Sun and Moon Potion

Here is a powerful herbal healing essence you can make in one week's time. For an immune system boost, crush a mixture of equal parts rosemary, sandalwood and the petals of a red carnation. Place the crushed herbs in a colored class jar filled with virgin olive oil. After seven days' storage on a windowsill so as to be exposed to both Sun and Moon, strain and place the infused oil back into the jar. You now have a hearty supply of homemade healing oil to use in the bath, or to rub on your pulse points: temple, wrists, backs of knees, and behind the ears. As soon as you feel rundown, one application should make a difference.

Astrological Almanac – Green Witchery Wisdom

Plants carry potent energy you can use to amplify your magical workings. Use the signs of the sun, moon and stars to your advantage and, over time, you will come to know which ones are most effective for you. Make sure to use your own astrological chart in working with these herbs. Here is a guide to the astrological associations of plants you may grow in your kitchen garden or keep dried in your pantry:

Aries, ruled by Mars: carnation, cedar, clove, cumin, fennel, juniper, peppermint and pine.

Taurus, ruled by Venus: apple, daisy, lilac, magnolia, oak moss, orchid, plumeria, rose, thyme, tonka bean, vanilla and violet.

Gemini, ruled by Mercury: almond, bergamot, mint, clover, dill, lavender, lemongrass, lily and parsley.

Cancer, ruled by the Moon: eucalyptus, gardenia, jasmine, lemon, lotus, rose, myrrh and sandalwood.

Leo, ruled by the Sun: acacia, cinnamon, heliotrope, nutmeg, orange and rosemary.

Virgo, ruled by Mercury: almond, cypress, bergamot, mint, mace, moss, thyme and patchouli.

Libra, ruled by Venus: catnip, marjoram, mugwort, spearmint, sweet pea, thyme and vanilla.

Scorpio, ruled by Pluto: allspice, basil, cumin, galangal and ginger.

Sagittarius, ruled by Jupiter: anise, cedar wood, sassafras, star anise and honeysuckle.

Capricorn, ruled by Saturn: lemon thyme, mimosa, vervain and vetiver.

Aquarius, ruled by Uranus: gum, citron, cypress, lavender, spearmint and pine.

Pisces, ruled by Neptune: clover, orris, neroli, sarsaparilla and sweet pea.

Conclusion

Serious Moonlight

Since prehistory, we have looked into the night sky with wonder. The moon is both magical and majestic. She rules the ocean tides, the crops in our fields and our moods and emotions. The moon is mysterious and reflective. Aside from the sun, our brightest star and the source of life, the moon is the single-most important light in our sky. Every culture in the world, both past and present, has moon lore, myths, rites and a great respect for our favorite "night light." The early Babylonians called the moon "the boat of life," while the Taoist Chinese believed the moon was a white dragon. A most unusual perspective came from the usually reasonable Plutarch, who theorized that girls grew into women as a result of a female essence that came down from the moon. The very name of our galaxy, the Milky Way, comes from the mythical white cow that jumped over the moon. It may well be that no other celestial object is as revered as the moon. A common and beloved ritual—baking, decorating, and eating a birthday cake—is descended from the Greek custom of celebrating the monthly birthday of the moon goddess Artemis with full-moon cakes.

To this day, modern Pagans "draw down the moon" in some rituals. In Asia, it is said that the moon is the mirror that reflects everything in the world. Some cultures consider the moon to be male and the sun female: for example, the Japanese honor the sun goddess Amaterasu and her brother the moon god Tsukiyomi. In this book we have explored some of the myths and lore of the moon, supplying you with many approaches to ritual from the treasury of our human history. Let Luna be your guide as you design and develop your own moon ceremonies and rites of the night.

About the Author

Cerridwen Greenleaf is the author of Running Press' wildly popular *Witches' Spellbook* series. The author of Chronicle Books' *Good Spells* series and rituals for life, she has worked with many of the leading lights of the Wiccan world, including Starhawk, Z Budapest, Eileen Holland, Christopher Penzack, Ray Buckland, John Michael Greer, Luisah Teish and many more. Greenleaf's graduate work in medieval studies has given her deep insight into ancient magic, making her work unique in the field. Her latest series for Running Press, *The Witches' Spell Book* series, has sold over 100,000 copies and her latest collection, *The Book of Kitchen Witchery*, is inspired by her popular blog, *Your Magical Home*.

Bibliography

Ahlquist, Cynthia. *Llewellyn's Magical Almanac.* St Paul: Llewellyn, 1996.

Budapest, Zsusanna. *The Holy Book of Women's Mysteries.* Berkeley: Wingbow, 1980.

Bulfinch, Thomas. *Bulfinch's Mythology.* New York: Modern Library, 1998.

Cicero, Marcus Tullius. *De Natura Deorum: The Nature of the Gods.* New York: Viking Press, 1985.

Cunningham, Nancy Brady. *A Book of Women's Altars.* Bottom: Red Wheel, 2002.

Driver, Tom. *The Magic of Ritual.* San Francisco: HarperSanFrancisco, 1991.

Eliade, Mircea. *Rites and Symbols of Initiation.* Dallas: Spring Publications, 1958.

Elk, Black. *Black Elk Speaks.* Lincoln: Bison Books, 2003.

Etheridge, J. W. *Targum of Onkelos and Jonathan Ben Uzziel on the Pentateuch with the Fragments of the Jerusalem from the Chaldee.* Hoboken: KTAV Press, 1969.

Fitch, Ed (published as Herman Slater). *A Book of Pagan Rituals.* York Beach: Weiser, 1978.

Frazer, James. *The Golden Bough.* New York: Avenel, 1981.

Gardner, Gerald. *The Meaning of Witchcraft.* Boston: Weiser, 2004.

Graves, Robert. *The White Goddess.* New York: Noonday Press, 1966.

Heerens Lysne, Robin. *Living a Sacred Life.* Berkeley: Conari Press, 1999.

Huizinga, Johan. *The Autumn of the Middle Ages.* Chicago: University of Chicago Press, 1997.

Kingma, Daphne Rose. *Weddings from the Heart.* Berkeley: Conari Press, 1994.

Knight, Brenda. *Gem Magic.* Gloucester: Fair Winds Press, 2004.

Mandela, Nelson. *Long Walk to Freedom.* Boston: Back Bay Books, 1995.

McKenna, Terence. *True Hallucinations.* San Francisco: HarperCollins, 1993.

Mongahan, Patricia. *The Book of Goddesses & Heroines.* St Paul: Llewellyn, 2004.

Rappaport, Roy. *Ritual and Religion in the Making of Humanity.* Boston: Cambridge University, 1999.

Roberts-Gallagher, Kim. *Daily Planetary Guide.* St. Paul: Llewellyn, 2004.

Silverwind, Selene. "Pagan Children and Ethics." *The Blessed Bee,* 2003

Smith, Steven. *Wylundt's Book of Incense.* York Beach: Weiser, 1989.

Teish, Luisah. *Jump Up.* Berkeley: Conari, 2000.

Walker, Barbara. *The Woman's Dictionary of Symbols and Sacred Objects.* San Francisco: Harper and Row, 1998.

Walker, Barbara. *Women's Rituals.* San Francisco: Harper and Row, 1986.